Difficulties for Christian Belief

Difficulties
for Christian Belief

Edited by

R. P. C. HANSON

MACMILLAN

London · Melbourne · Toronto

ST MARTIN'S PRESS

New York

1967

© Macmillan and Co. 1967

MACMILLAN AND COMPANY LIMITED
Little Essex Street London WC 2
also Bombay Calcutta Madras Melbourne

THE MACMILLAN COMPANY OF CANADA LIMITED
70 Bond Street Toronto 2

ST MARTIN'S PRESS INC
175 Fifth Avenue New York NY 10010

Library of Congress catalog card no. 67–10580

Printed in Great Britain by
WESTERN PRINTING SERVICES LTD., BRISTOL

Contents

Acknowledgement

THE permission of Hodder & Stoughton is gratefully acknowledged to reproduce arguments already printed in *Faith and Philosophy* (1966).

Introduction

LONG-RANGE weather forecasts are notoriously un-certain, even in these days; to indulge, therefore, in predictions about the changes in the theological climate likely to take place in the next fifty years would be a hazardous and unprofitable activity. But a short-range weather forecast, or at least an account of the theological climate as it is today and as it is likely to remain tomorrow (not to speak of later dates), is a task well within the powers of ordinary human intelligence. The main characteristic of the theological climate at the moment appears to be uncertainty. The modern theological student finds his confidence in the Christian faith threatened from at least two directions. The traditional reasons for believing in God are being strongly questioned and the reliability of the Gospels' accounts of Jesus has been seriously shaken. Both natural religion and revealed religion seem to be under fire. The inability of contemporary philosophy to find any place for metaphysics, and the very widespread conviction that science alone can discover knowledge that is genuinely knowledge and not illusion or fancy, have combined to remove from the philosophy of religion many (but not all) of its traditional supports. Between religion and science there appears to many to be not so much an antagonism as a gulf. They appear to be speaking of quite different things and for many people the difference is simply that science is speaking about objective reality and religion about subjective illusion. Some students of theology can exist on revealed religion alone, that is, they can be content with the witness of the Bible without seeking to relate it to the world as it is known to us apart from what the Bible says to us. But this is not possible for all. For many the vital question still remains, whether we can understand the God of the Bible without first having some idea of what the word 'God' means. This is precisely what the present debate among the philosophers and theologians is about—the meaning (if any) of the word 'God'.

On another front an uncertainty quite as serious prevails. The historical career of Jesus Christ is not, of course, the whole of the Christian religion, but it is difficult to deny that it is at the centre of it. We have outlived the days when everybody tried to write a life of Jesus Christ, beginning with the modest but significant *Ecce Homo* by J. R. Seeley in 1865 and ending perhaps when Hall Caine's vast *Life of Christ* dropped dead from the printing-press in the nineteen-thirties. But it is reasonable to suppose that most thinking people would assume that the details of the life and teaching of Jesus

Christ were of the highest importance for the Christian faith. The development of historical criticism of the Gospels has now reached a point where to many these details seem to be beyond recovery. It is not that anyone seriously doubts the historical existence of Jesus Christ. On the contrary, the 'Christ-myth' theories have long been abandoned by almost all scholars. But the uncertainty lies in achieving the distinction between what Jesus Christ did and said on the one hand, and on the other what the early Church said that he did and said. Our only authority for his deeds and words is the writers of the early Church, and it is quite clear that in some cases the evangelists altered the tradition that had come down to them or were handling material that had itself been drastically altered or edited before it reached them. If this is true (as it certainly is) of some cases, why not of all, or of nearly all? How do we distinguish Jesus from the Church's interpretation of Jesus? We need not oppose them to each other, nor reject one in favour of the other, but must we not distinguish them? This task has recently become so difficult for students of the New Testament that some have nearly given it up in despair, and almost claim that not only is it impossible to disentangle the historical Jesus from the Jesus of the Church's preaching, but that it is undesirable to do so. It is doubtful, however, whether this argument is likely to impress for long either the man in the pew or the theological student in the lecture-room.

In addition to these uncertainties, another uncertainty prevails about the resurrection. All the old doubts that haunted the generation of Bishop Gore, and caused a deeper shade of melancholy to invest his grave, bearded face as each close friend confessed these doubts to him, have risen up again to trouble our generation. Here science and history join hands to shake confidence in this central Christian belief. All the old arguments are brought up; very few new historical considerations have been added. But the subject has been given a new sharpness and relevance as a result of the central place that the resurrection occupies in the programme of 'demythologizing' proposed by Bultmann, who allows full weight to the difficulties of establishing the resurrection as an event in history. The doubt that his interpretation appears to raise about the status of the resurrection has far-reaching consequences. Almost everybody grants that some reinterpretation of traditional Christian doctrines is necessary. Can we demythologize the resurrection? If the early Christians really believed that heaven was a spatial territory high up in the sky and hell a large series of caverns in the middle of the earth (though it is doubtful if they did), then clearly these concepts must be reinterpreted. If they believed that the world was going to end very shortly with a Second Coming envisaged in terms of traditional Jewish apocalyptic (and they certainly did), then this belief must be reinterpreted. In fact, it can be seen to be undergoing a reinterpretation in the New Testament itself. We may demythologize the Ascension, and the belief in demon-possession, but how far is this process to go? Should it embrace the belief in an Atonement? Should it reinterpret the New Testament idea of sacrifice? Once again, can we demythologize the resurrection? To leave these questions unanswered serves to deepen contemporary theological uncertainty.

The final uncertainty concerns the shape, the authority, and the appearance of the Church. Sixty years ago most advanced and liberal scholars would have doubted the necessity of the Church in any form. When von Hügel addressed the Religious Thought Society in London in 1913, with W. R. Inge in the chair, he had to begin his defence of the Church as an institution by assuming that almost everybody present saw no necessity for the existence of the Church. We are not quite in the same situation today. The work of Biblical scholarship in the intervening period has at least served to show the utter impossibility of divorcing the Church from the Gospel, and has established the unalterably central position that the Church occupies in the whole Christian dispensation. And the Ecumenical Movement has fixed in the minds of many the conviction that there is in some sense one Church to which all Christians belong and that its form could be recovered. But to this Church as God designed it, to this Church described in such glowing terms in the New Testament, the empirical, local Church of our day offers a melancholy contrast. It seems so much preoccupied with matters that are not central, so deplorably bourgeois, late-Victorian, and middle class in its structure, ethos, and outlook. Its leaders appear to be obsessed with administration and either uninterested in doctrine or afraid of it. Its ministers and its representative assemblies seem to be gripped by the ideas and preoccupations of the last generation, not this one. Its pastoral life seems to be feeble, dispirited, and ineffective. If a contemporary theology can be found, how can it function as the inspiration of so uninviting an organism as this?

The outlook for theology is not, however, wholly discouraging. The very fact that so much questioning is taking place has its advantages. A new openness and flexibility in theological thought are everywhere evident. All possibilities are liable to be explored; the most radical critical and destructive, certainly, but also possibilities that are positive and likely to lead to the rehabilitation of Christianity. When all the fences are taken down in a town, then everybody can see everybody else's garden. Today we are witnessing a genuine Scholars' International, a situation when theologians of all disciplines and all traditions and all denominations can meet on equal terms, not because they are conservatives timidly encountering liberals, or Roman Catholics carefully unbending to Protestants, but because they are all scholars bent on exploring the significance and unravelling the history of Christianity. Strange and welcome cross-bench attitudes are appearing. Roman Catholics are writing books warmly appreciative of Calvin, Luther, and Wesley. Baptists are devoting volumes to demonstrating the need for regarding baptism as a sacrament. French Calvinists are extolling the eucharist as a sacrifice. Thomists are joining hands with existentialists. With this new openness goes a welcome new rigour in theological study. Theology has now become a very professional and high-pressure subject. It is impossible any longer for the amateur to succeed in it. In the early years of this century W. R. Inge could be asked to write the volume on St. John's Gospel for the International Critical Commentary Series, and could be offered Divinity professorships at both Oxford and Cambridge, without his knowing any Hebrew. Today this would be impossible. Teutonic thoroughness has captured the whole field of theology; study and research must be conducted with an accuracy and comprehensiveness never achieved before. The would-be scholar must assimilate a large range of literature on his subject in at least English, German, and French, before he dares to write about it himself. He must exclude no fact or theory from his review just because it is awkward or disturbing or unorthodox. And this applies to the orthodoxy of the radicals as much as to orthodoxy of the conservatives. If we look today at the blinkers in which Newman set out to analyse the history of early Christian doctrine or Pusey to expound the book of Daniel, we find them absurd. But we find equally absurd the selective account of the origins of the early

Church given in E. W. Barnes's *The Rise of Christianity* (1947) or the version of the life of Jesus given in *The Nazarene Gospel Restored* (1953), by R. R. Graves and J. Podro. Openness, interchange of different traditions, and a wholesome rigour in pursuing research have never done Christianity any harm, and we may confidently predict that out of this ferment, this many-voiced pursuit of the scent of truth by the hounds of scholarship, will emerge in the end lasting good, even though it be at the cost of pain and heart-searching.

One curious phenomenon, which should perhaps give comfort to the dispirited student of theology, is the interest everywhere evident in the study of this subject. The churches are apparently emptying. The number of candidates for the ordained ministry is dwindling. But the number of people who want to study theology at institutes of higher education and of those who read books about theology increases steadily. Over the last twenty years more and more universities in this country—secular universities in no way tied to any denomination—have set up Departments of Theology. On the Continent it is reported that publishers cannot find enough manuscripts to publish in order to satisfy the demand for books on theology. With the increased emphasis on the role of the laity evident in all the major denominations has gone a suggestion, still faint but increasing in volume, that perhaps the laity might be interested in theology, might be capable of understanding it, teaching it, and even preaching it. It may be that we are heading for a situation in which the local teachers will be better qualified in theology than the local clergy in many parts of this country. If theology has to undergo a reinterpretation, it may simultaneously experience a laicization. It might be that both processes will be for its ultimate good.

Paradoxical though it may seem, then, the student of theology is in the position of General Foch, who is reported to have declared in an order of the day, 'My centre is giving way, my right is in retreat; situation excellent. I shall attack!' The subject with which theology deals is, after all, the Christian faith and the Christian Church; the two are inseparable; one is the expression of the other. It is undeniable that men have believed in God as revealed in Christ, and that men do so, even now. The existence of faith is a stubborn fact, a contemporary phenomenon. If anyone will take the trouble to penetrate beneath the unattractive surface of the Church today, he will find men and women who are living a distinctively Christian life in the power of Christian faith. They are not all elderly or middle-aged; they are not all weak-minded nor very ill; they are not all romantic anti-quarians living in cathedral towns. Some of them are scientists and technologists; some of them are shop-stewards and garage mechanics and lorry-drivers. It may well be that there are peculiar difficulties in the way of Christian belief today, but Christians do believe. We have among us the phenomenon of Christianity as a living religion. How did this come about? What is there that makes it live, even in the twentieth century? The writer of the last of the essays in this book opens by pointing out to the reader that in one sense all the preceding essays have in different ways put the onus of justifying Christianity on the existence and activity of the Church. He is quite right. In some sort of mysterious way Christianity works for many people; it satisfies; it makes sense. Theology is a discipline that does not operate upon a purely hypothetical subject, but on something that has a concrete expression. Theology is the rational consideration and investigation of that concretely expressed subject, and the activity of vindicating it to reason where and if it can be vindicated and modifying it where and if it should be modified. But the strange thing is there to be studied, inherited from past ages and marked by the movements and vicissitudes of those ages, yet still alive today.

This book is about doctrine, that is about an intermediate field, between the direct study of the Bible on the one hand and the direct application of Christianity to contemporary society on the other. It is neither Bible-study nor preaching. It is thrown designedly into that vast gulf that yawns between the lecture-room and the pulpit, in the hope that its debris may contribute towards building up a causeway across the gulf. In the opinion of the writers, there is no part of Christian thought where help is more needed today, and it was in fact at the request of the students of the Christian Association of the University of Nottingham that the substance of this book was first given, in the form of a series of lectures delivered in the University in the autumn of 1965. The lectures were addressed to two different groups, both of whom were represented in the audiences: to clergy, who tend not to see any difficulties for Christian belief, and to students interested in theology, who tend to see nothing else. Clergy have in too many cases given up reading ten or twenty or thirty years ago. As an experienced botanist can tell the age of a tree by inspecting the rings on a cross-section of its trunk, or an experienced geologist can tell the age of a group of rocks by looking at their stratification, so an experienced theologian can tell the year in which a minister of religion was ordained by looking at his library and noting exactly when he gave up reading. On the other hand students are at an impressionable age when every latest radical theory tends to look like incontrovertible fact and ideas exercise a disproportionate influence compared with life and experience. These essays are an attempt to appeal to both groups at the same time. They endeavour to deal honestly with the difficulties that do in truth face Christian belief today. They are intended to rouse from complacency any who think that commending Christianity in the nineteen-sixties is a simple, straightforward affair, demanding no more than a statement in plain terms of the traditional Gospel. And they are intended to show the radically-minded that even professional theologians can be as radically-minded as they, and though they may not know all the answers they have at any rate thought of most of the objections. On the other hand, the book is intended to exemplify a conviction, shared by all the contributors to it, that Christianity does not consist only of objections, but that there are positive and constructive reasons for believing in it and that no student and no clergyman need despair either of belief or of the means of commending belief.

Perhaps two more groups for whom this book is designed should be mentioned. One is theological students. For too long it has been widely assumed among those who train theological students that all that is necessary is that the student should be as well grounded as possible in the historical criticism of the Old and New Testaments, should know something about the history of early Christian doctrine, and be given some training in the technique of sermon preparation, or of teaching, and that he can then be trusted to preach the Christian faith from the pulpit or teach it in the classroom. That this assumption is wrong can be easily discovered by anybody who likes to listen to the average sermon or to the Scripture lesson in the average school. In this country the subject of Christian doctrine has been in recent years largely avoided, partly no doubt because those who should be teaching it and those who should be writing about it did not know what to say. The other group is the ordinary intelligent layman outside the University who has no desire to abandon his religion and who is not afraid to face criticism of the Christian faith and the demand to accept a reinterpretation of it. He exists in larger numbers than perhaps either the defenders or the opponents of Christianity are aware.

The staff of the Department of Theology of the University of Nottingham consists of six full-time and two or three part-time members teaching about sixty students all told. But it inherits a tradition, which it is anxious to maintain worthily, of producing joint works. In 1958 there appeared *A Guide to the Scrolls*, with the sub-title 'Nottingham Studies on Qumran Discoveries', edited by A. R. C. Leaney, and in 1963 *Four Anchors from the Stern*, with the sub-title 'Nottingham Reactions to Recent Cambridge Essays', edited by Alan Richardson. The contributors to *Difficulties for Christian Belief* can only hope that their volume will receive the same kind welcome as was accorded to its two predecessors from the same birthplace.

R. P. C. H.

1: *Belief in God*

J. RICHMOND

THIS essay is about *difficulties*; it is in no sense an exposition of classical Christian belief in God. That is, it is not a lecture on Christian doctrine. If parts of it appear to be negative, even pessimistic, this must necessarily be the case, because we are concentrating upon difficulties and dilemmas. Moreover, the essay is not about particular difficulties of concern to this or that specialist group; it is not about psychological or sociological difficulties, for example. Rather, it is about universal difficulties that concern thinking men on as wide an international front as we can conceive of. It is about difficulties that are such for our time and world situation. Unless I am sadly mistaken, the doctrine of God is a peculiarly troublesome one for our time both outside and inside the Christian communion. While it is true that a great many secular Western men are puzzled and perplexed by belief in God, it is inside the Christian Churches today that we hear of 'Godless Christianity', that we hear that 'God is no more', that we are told of 'the end of theism'. I take it for granted then, that the doctrine of God is a perplexing one not only for those unsympathetic towards religious belief, but for many of those who embrace it with warmth and affection. Here, in this essay, I can only hope to show what the real and pressing problems are, and to speculate about the ways in which they might be resolved.

I make no apology for the method I have chosen to follow, which is an unashamedly *historical* one. It is based upon my conviction that a perplexing and confused present situation can only be illuminated if we inquire about its origins in the past; that is, the only way to understand the present is to look at it in the light cast upon it by the past.

But the investigation of a fairly recent past throws us into a slightly more remote past, and so on. My own view is that our main contemporary theological difficulties (like many of our economic, political, and social ones) are rooted in the second half of the eighteenth century, and that some of the roots even stretch back to the beginning of the sixteenth.

Let us then glance at the historical background of contemporary theology. Many historians of theological thought would agree that much of our modern theology was founded in the period that lasted approximately from 1600 to 1750. Theologically, we owe to this period more perhaps than we realize. The main characteristic of the theology of this period (so far as belief in God is concerned) can be put in this way: by and large, belief in God was commended and defended as a *metascientific theory*[1] necessitated by the existence and structure of nature. This was sometimes expounded by insisting that the sheer existence of nature required belief in an Author of Nature, a First Cause, an Unmoved Mover of all things identifiable with the God of historic Hebrew–Christian belief. It was also expounded by insisting that the structure of nature necessitated belief in a Cosmic Designer or Architect, identifiable with the deity of Hebrew–Christian religion. Most dubiously of all, it was occasionally suggested that the gaps in the human understanding of nature were, so to speak, providentially deliberate; that these corresponded to mysterious irregularities and

[1] By a 'metascientific theory' here is meant a *metascientific* explanation, which asserts that a purely scientific explanation of external reality is inadequate, and that it needs to be completed or supplemented by one that uses theological categories lying beyond ordinary empirical observation. Such an explanation cannot be either verified or falsified by those procedures that are ordinarily used in the testing of scientific explanations. Such an explanation can therefore be said to go beyond the evidence available to the sciences. Metascientific theology can, therefore, be defined as a type that moulds itself upon or imitates scientific method, introduces a concept such as 'God' by relating God to nature, or asserts that nature is ultimately inexplicable without the introduction of such a concept. Occasionally it took the form of introducing theological categories (such as 'God' or 'design') into gaps in scientific understanding.

gaps in the functions and movements of nature, gaps into which the divine activity could be introduced.

In an age when the main lines of the natural sciences were being laid down (and when these sciences were making fantastic progress), when the minds of Europeans were concentrated on physical nature above all else, it is at least intelligible why the attempt should be made to commend belief in God by establishing his structural relation to nature. Increasingly throughout the period, God became an object with a *function* in relationship to a reality conceived of as mathematical and mechanical. In these ways belief in God was considered necessary for rational, thinking men during the period. Here then we have the emergence of modern Christian *natural theology* —a set of metascientific proofs, arguments, or demonstrations leading to the necessary existence of God.

We must notice two things about the natural theology of the period. The first is that if ever it could be shown that nature is explicable without the introduction of the concept 'God', the theological edifice erected on the basis of this natural theology might very well collapse. Secondly, if it could be shown that reason could not with a high degree of certainty establish God's existence (a European conviction that went back as far as Plato), it is clear that a most grave crisis would follow.

In fact, in the next period that we consider, from approximately 1750 to 1800, this is very much what happened. In the critical work of thinkers like David

Hume and Immanuel Kant we find a most searching critique of the traditional theistic demonstrations and arguments (leading to natural theology).

Such criticism appeared to show (at the very least) that there was a great deal of evidence against the conclusions of these arguments. It showed, certainly, that the theistic demonstrations were no longer compelling, no longer coercive. It did not, as it is sometimes said, 'demolish' the older natural theology; but it certainly undermined men's confidence in it. Also, in the same period there occurred rapid developments in the empirical sciences. Gaps in men's understanding of the physical cosmos were being gradually filled in, a process that was of course to continue throughout the nineteenth century and is continuing today. Such intellectual processes led inevitably to the disclaimer of Laplace, that he no longer required 'God' as a scientific hypothesis.

This intellectual crisis was the crisis of the Enlightenment, the crisis in the light of which we must read modern theology. The lack of an appreciation of the significance of this crisis would make much modern theology a closed book to us. In the modern period, say from 1800 until the present day, how has theology reacted to the crisis of the Enlightenment? It is dangerous to generalize, but perhaps we can say this much. In Catholic circles, and in other Anglo-American conservative circles, the attempt was made to overcome the scepticism of the Enlightenment and to rehabilitate natural theology along fairly familiar lines. In Protestant circles, and this is seen most clearly in the sphere of German Protestant theology, theologians conceded fairly quickly that Europeans had lost their nerve about studying natural theology in the old ways. Consequently, post-Enlightenment Protestant theology has exhibited, and to a large extent still exhibits, certain significant characteristics.

Three of these are particularly important. First, there was reluctance to regard theological concepts and symbols (such as 'God' for example) as metascientific explanatory categories. Secondly, there was a strong tendency to deny that the context of theological thinking is physical nature. Rather, it was insisted that that which stands over against man, that which is to be known, is a reality other than nature, or rather, a reality that greatly transcends nature. This was, it can be said, an antinaturalistic tendency. Thirdly, and this was perhaps the most significant characteristic of all, there emerged a radically altered conception of *man*, of the *human*. A revolution was set in motion against the Cartesian conception of man as *Res cogitans* (thinking substance), as a being whose essence can be identified with his ability to think. There emerged a picture of man as a being whose total nature greatly transcended the pure, abstract knower of the natural sciences.

What do these three characteristics of modern, post-Enlightenment theology add up to? They add up to something like this: the starting-point of theology, of the

science or doctrine of God, is *man* himself. Theology is a
discipline that begins with the human (not with physical,
external, objective nature) and works 'outwards', so to
speak, from there. This is the conception of theology as an
anthropological (its critics would say *anthropocentric*)
science. One believes in God, first by believing in man, in
the human. But how, in practice, did this anthropological
approach work out? How in fact did theologians approach
the doctrine of God through the doctrine of man? Let me
sketch extremely briefly several significant post-Enlightenment trends or movements that began, as I have
said, with man, and moved from man towards God.

First, there have been theologies beginning from man's
inner *religious* awareness and experience. This type of
theological approach began very early in the nineteenth
century, continued right through it, and perhaps reached
its culmination in Rudolf Otto's highly influential book
Das Heilige (*The Idea of the Holy*). It could not in-
appropriately be styled a *descriptive* approach—the
technical label is *phenomenological*. It consisted of profound, detailed analyses of human personality, pointing
to the widespread primal awareness in man of the super-
sensible, the numinous, the tremendous, an awareness
held to be one of the strongest roots of the world-histori-
cal religions. In tendency, of course, this approach
sharply denied that man was exhaustively definable as a
piece of *thinking substance*, as the bare, abstract knower of
the sciences. And, of course, Christian systematic theo-

logians attempted to show that man's distinctively *religious* structure found its completion and fulfilment in a distinctively Christian context of belief, worship, and practice.

Secondly, there have been theologies beginning from man's *moral* awareness and experience. Clearly, this tendency stems from Kant's attempt to rehabilitate religious belief on moral grounds. Here the assertion is made that man's main context is not the sphere of nature but the realm of moral values and ideals. The purely 'natural' sciences appear to be indifferent to these. Much was made within this approach of how values are related to man; of how (to quote one philosopher who influenced this type of theology, Nicolai Hartmann) 'values press upon man for their own actualization'; of how 'moral values take a sort of personal interest in and indulge in activity towards their own realization in human life'. The effect of such thinking on theology was impressive; it was insisted that man's nature, as invaded by the pressure of values making absolute and unconditional demands, pointed towards man's knowledge of and derivation from some transcendent sphere. Here again, Christian systematic theologians tried to show that man's essentially moral structure found its completion and fulfilment within a distinctively religious context.

Thirdly, there have been theologies beginning from man's distinctively *historical* experience. This approach to theology stems, I suppose, from the work of thinkers

like Wilhelm Dilthey in Germany and R. G. Colling-
wood in England. Here again we find the rather sharp
denial that the main context of human life is nature.
Rather, we find the insistence that man lives within the
dimension of *history*. History is sharply distinguished
from nature because history is the sphere of the distinctively *human*. In his historical experience and investiga-
tions man encounters humanity, humanity as a rich
reality that encounters him, humanity that lives on in the
present, in documents, monuments, texts, creeds, con-
fessions, and deeds. This reality is one that informs,
questions, corrects, enriches and judges man. Theologically, there is the denial that theological concepts like
'God' are matascientific ones, deriving from man's attempts to comprehend the origin, structure or function, of
nature. Rather, it is insisted that they are terms that can
only be grasped within the context of a long, complex,
and continuing, process of commitment, obedience, and
reflection, in which all kinds of experience (moral,
religious, affective, and intellectual) have been sifted,
evaluated, and interpreted. Here again, Christian systematic theologians have made much of this dimension of
history in the interpretation of their materials.

Fourthly, and finally, there have been theologies beginning from man's understanding of human existence.
'Existence' is here used in the rather technical sense
given to it by the philosophical school of existentialism,
which has been in our time such a potent influence on

theology. I suppose that the basic tenet of existentialist thought has been the sharp denial that man exists as do the objects and processes of nature. More particularly, man is not a finished, completed, finalized, shaped, or realized substance or thing. Rather, and more positively, man can be said to be essentially a future being; man is never anything, he is always potentially something; or, we can say, man is always possibility. Man lives wrongly (or as existentialists would prefer to say, inauthentically, falsely) when he understands himself as a natural thing that is finalized or realized. Man's main task is therefore to move from false to true existence, to transcend the world of nature, the sphere of process and law, to grasp his future, authentic self. Clearly, the effect of this type of thinking on theology has been both far-reaching and impressive. And again Christian systematic theologians have tried to reformulate their materials within a distinctively existential framework.

Within these anthropological or humanistic approaches we have the emergence of a picture of man and reality that differs sharply from that presupposed by the sciences. This is a picture that denies that man is merely a finalized piece of thinking substance; a picture of man as a creature aware of the numinous, aware of absolute demand being laid upon him, aware that what he is and what he thinks are (partly at least) constituted by history, aware that his real existence, from which in his empirical reality he is estranged, is one that lies before him in the future. And conversely, the dimension within which man lives and knows is depicted as greatly transcending the dimension of nature; man also lives within a realm of values, within the dimension of history, within the context of existence. That is, belief in God appears to make sense within this distinctively human framework, in which man, as an essentially moral, religious, historical, and existential creature, is aware of a realm of values, is conscious of demand laid upon him to realize his true self, and grasps that what is real and significant for him is mediated partly through that history of which he is a part.

Nevertheless, it cannot be concealed that difficulties and problems do remain, and in plenty. Three of them can be noticed here. First, one set of contemporary problems arises out of the differences between Christians over the whole business of *theological method*. There is evidence that world-wide research is being prosecuted into the so-called *methodology* of theology. It is true I, think, that confusion over this lies behind much of the theological turmoil of the nineteen-sixties. By the methodology of theology I mean the discussion of questions like these: what is the starting-point of theology? where do we begin? how is theology possible? The turmoil indicates that there are still choices to be made. In this lecture I have indicated two starting-points: nature and man. What choice, for instance, can we make between these two? Can theology return to nature as a starting point?

In our day the temptation to do so is clearly enormous.

My own view, for what it is worth, is that theology ought not, and indeed cannot. Contemporary thought makes it clear that this is a dangerous way for theology to begin. An example of such contemporary thought is modern analytic philosophy, which contains within itself certain insights inherited from the logical positivism that was so popular during the nineteen-twenties and thirties. Despite positivism's alarming and overt hostility to all forms of theological thinking, it nevertheless performed certain valuable functions for theology. For example, by its studies of a comparison of the language of theology with the language of physics, in which it was shown that in the language of physics meaning and verifiability are so closely interwoven as to be almost indistinguishable, positivism demonstrated that whatever religious beliefs are, they are not some kind of metascientific theory or hypotheses of an explanatory kind. Positivism made it clear that religion and science are two very different things indeed. In fact, such analysis has heavily under-scored Enlightenment criticisms of religious beliefs presented as hypotheses or theories that might correct, or supplement, or inform, or compete with scientific attempts to understand nature. For this reason alone, I would urge that this approach to the doctrine of God is one fraught with difficulties and dangers. My own view is that a viable approach to religious belief is an anthropological one, beginning with man, with *humanitas* in the widest possible sense.

Secondly, it may be said that modern man is perhaps singularly uninterested in absolute moral obligation, in his history, in the problems and quandaries of human existence. This may well be true; but in reply it may be asked if it is not just these characteristics of modern man that are so terrifying. The possibility of belief in God is obviously linked with the attempt to undermine this depersonalization, this dehistoricization, against which not only theologians but also philosophers and prophets have raged in modern times. If the view of theology we have outlined here is tenable, then there must be a sense in which theology must stand or fall with man, with *humanitas*.

Thirdly, there is a final difficulty, which may be the most important of all. I have described theology as an anthropological discipline; it takes *humanitas* as its starting-point. There is therefore a sense in which it shares common problems with the other humanities. And these problems are universal, worldwide, and the concern of us all. The fundamental problem of this group has, in my opinion, been neatly formulated recently by Ernest Gellner.[1]

Gellner points to 'the chasm between that which is science and that which is not'. Unless one sees the chasm one cannot understand the crisis. Or he can describe the

[1] See his essay, 'The Crisis in the Humanities and the Mainstream of Philosophy', in *Crisis in the Humanities*, ed. J. H. Plumb, pp. 45–81.

roots of the crisis by speaking of 'the towering superiority of science as a source of knowledge about the universe'. He comes to the heart of our problem when he formulates it thus: 'how are the concepts in terms of which we see ourselves and live our lives to be related to those we take seriously as genuine knowledge of this world?' He can put it another way: 'the language of the humanities is incomparably closer to what we *are*, to the life we live, than is the language of science; but on the other hand it is not obvious that the humanities contain, in any serious sense, genuine *knowledge*'.

Now if Gellner is right, and I am inclined to think that he probably is, the consequences for theology are these. Supposing that it is granted that the religious man is justified, on the grounds of his understanding of *humanitas*, in believing in God—that is, in interpreting his life as God-given and God-destined—can he go on from there to make assertions *about* the nature of all reality as such? Can he, on the basis of his belief, go on to make descriptive affirmations *about* the world, *about* the universe? To use technical language, can he go on to claim that religious belief is *cognitive*? Can he say that religion concerns *knowing* as well as *being*? At this point there is again perplexing confusion among theologians. Unless I am mistaken, some of these are apparently prepared to concede that religion cannot seriously claim to yield knowledge *about* reality, to be cognitive; they appear to be prepared to reduce religion merely to a way of life, a set of perspectives, insights, or motivations, without which our *humanitas* would be gravely impoverished.

My own view is that theology ought not to make any such concession, unless it wants to commit suicide. Rather, *the* task facing theology today is to show how the knowledge of man casts light on all being as such. It is to draw lines from man outwards, so to speak, so that these lines point firmly towards those aspects of reality to which religion has always drawn attention and from which it has nourished itself. This, I dare to say, is the task that faces theologians and the Churches today. But it is a task that will not be accomplished in one essay, nor in a week; it is one that will require the labours of a theological generation, a great deal of hard work, much careful thinking, and detailed analysis. But to know what our task is is surely to be partly on the road to accomplishing it.

2: The Divinity of Jesus Christ

R. P. C. HANSON

I

IF a man were travelling in the eastern part of the
Roman Empire nineteen hundred years ago, and his
ship put in at a quay, a porter might ask to carry his bag-
gage, and would address him as *Kyrie*, 'Sir'. He might a
little later interview some customs official and address
him as *Kyrie*. As he walked about the town where he had
landed he would hear people discussing the latest news
concerning the Emperor, who might well be referred to
as *Kyrios* Caesar. He would pass the shrine of the Greek
god *Kyrios* Apollo. And he might meet a Jew who
would tell him that he worshipped *Kyrios* Sabaoth, the
Lord of Hosts. Only the last use of the word *Kyrios*
would refer to God as we use the term God. Similarly,
there were many different meanings of the word *theos*,

'god', in the ancient world. It could mean simply a man who was very good at impressing other people, honestly or fraudulently, or it could mean God Almighty, the one and only true God, and it could have several shades of meaning in between these two.

It is necessary to understand this before we approach the subject of the divinity of Jesus Christ, because it would be quite easy to show that the people of Jesus's day were ready to regard him as a very impressive person and to use the word *Kyrios*, and sometimes even perhaps the word *theos*, about him. But this is not the same thing as the traditional meaning of 'divinity'. We are all so much soaked in the Catholic tradition of theology that for us the word 'God' can only mean God Almighty, God as the only and sovereign God. Whether we like it or not, we are the heirs of Christian monotheism, and even if we are agnostics or atheists we are monotheistic agnostics or atheists. When we think about the divinity of Christ we mean the proposition that he was God in the fullest possible sense of that term, and when we examine the New Testament we must be sure that it is for this proposition that we are searching, and not for some lesser one. It might be quite easy to find a lesser statement. But can we find the greater one? What are the difficulties that beset this search?

Perhaps the greatest is the crudest. There is no doubt whatever that Jesus was a man, a human being with human passions and temptations, whose career we can date and place on its proper background. He was a Jew who lived from about A.D. 1 to 30 in Palestine, in Galilee and in Jerusalem. Nobody nowadays could, on the evidence of the first three Gospels, doubt that he existed and that he was, in every way that we can test him, a man. Could a man have gone round saying that he was God Almighty? Or if he did, was he sane? It is not uncommon for people to claim to be God Almighty, but they do not long remain outside mental hospitals. Nietszche did, for instance, at the end of his life, and so did Wagner at the end of his. But they both ended up under restraint. If one of our friends comes to us and confides that he has discovered that he is God Almighty, we naturally think that he is mad; and he is. Now, if Jesus really did proclaim or claim that he was God, it is most unlikely that anybody should have believed him, and we cannot blame them if they disbelieved.

Perhaps this is putting the matter too crudely. Perhaps it would be wiser to say that in orthodox preaching and teaching about Jesus the impression is often given that it was only occasionally that Jesus was to his contemporaries manifestly divine, when he performed miracles, for instance, or when he was transfigured, or when he gave his teaching. At other times he seemed human, not more than human. But even this picture is incredible to the realistic eye of the historically-minded twentieth-century reader. Jesus as the mysterious perambulating god, at times performing miracles and delivering oracles, and at other times doing his best, not very successfully, to appear normal, is obviously a figure of fiction. Nobody could ever have behaved like this, and nobody ever did. It is a simple truth of human experience that sane people, good people, people worthy to be imitated, just do not claim to be God.

Why, after all, should we want Jesus to be God? As civilized people living in the twentieth century and aware of historical perspective, we cannot help perceiving that primitive people, or members of societies less developed and less well informed and enlightened than ours, tend to attribute to God, as a kind of blank cheque, all phenomena that they do not understand. If Jesus was a very impressive teacher or an outstanding personality, it is very easy to imagine that the people of those remote centuries, ignorant and credulous, should have hailed him as God, because this was the highest compliment that they could pay him. But surely we can think of a better compliment that that, some category more realistic, more meaningful, and more in accord with contemporary thought. We can admire his character or his teaching, or the Christian ethic that he represented. We can take him as our exemplar or our ideal without going to the embarrassing and compromising length of calling him 'God'. To do this would be to take him out of his place in history and to put him into a category that means nothing to modern man and is positively uncongenial to contemporary philosophical thought. To the intellectual of our day, the divinity of Jesus Christ is not merely an embarrassment, it is positively a scandal. Would we not be doing a service to the cause of making Christianity acceptable to modern thought if we dropped this encumbering dogma?

The next fact that we must face is that it is not at all easy to prove from the evidence available that Jesus did himself really claim to be God Almighty. If we look at the first three Gospels, the Synoptic Gospels, no satisfactory evidence is forthcoming. He did indeed claim the power of forgiving sins and may have claimed to supersede the authority of Moses as expressed in the Law. He may have claimed to possess a new and special authority from God. But even if those concessions are made, this is still very far from claiming to be God Almighty. He may have claimed to be the Messiah, the Christ. Contemporary scholarship is very much divided upon this point. Many eminent scholars think that he never made this claim at all. But even if he did, there is no proof whatever that the Messiah was, in the Jewish view, God Almighty; on the contrary, he certainly was not. He may not even have been a superhuman figure. To appeal to the title 'Son of Man', so often applied to Jesus in the Synoptic Gospels, is worse than useless. Contemporary scholarship is in a state of utter confusion about this title. What did it mean, and, whatever it meant, did Jesus use it, and if he did, was he describing himself in using it, or somebody else? No clear answer can be given

to any of these questions. But it is wholly unlikely that if
and when they are resolved they will contribute to the
proof that Jesus claimed to be God. Anyway, there are
several strong indications in the Synoptic Gospels that
Jesus did not claim to be God. He prayed to his Father in
heaven. He alluded to God as his Father. On one occasion
he said, 'Why callest thou me good? There is none good
save God' (Mark x. 18), implying clearly that he was not
God. The fact that Matthew alters this sentence (Matt.
xix. 17) to remove this implication is all the more
damning evidence that the implication was there in Mark.

There is, of course, the Fourth Gospel, John's. Here
the prospect of proving that Jesus claimed to be God is
much brighter. In the Fourth Gospel Jesus talks almost
incessantly about his relations to God the Father, about
his Person and his significance, and he comes very close
indeed to claiming to be God. He utters such sayings as
'Before Abraham was, I am' (John viii. 58) and 'I and
the Father are one' (x. 30). He has everything clearly
arranged in his own mind: his mediating role, his divine
sonship, the resurrection, the coming of the Spirit, the
Church. The Fourth Gospel has always been the bastion
of those who wanted to prove from the Bible that Jesus
claimed to be God Almighty. But today that bastion has
fallen. It is almost impossible for serious scholarship today
to imagine that the Fourth Gospel gives us in most in-
stances the actual words of Jesus. The Jesus of the Fourth
Gospel is so utterly different a figure from the Jesus of

the Synoptic Gospels, so manifestly a developed picture, a later theological reconstruction, that it would be naïve or dishonest to pretend that we can rely on it for an accurate picture of what Jesus of Nazareth did originally claim for himself.

It should be pointed out that with this conclusion there collapses one of the most frequent and time-honoured arguments for the divinity of Jesus Christ, that which is summed up in the Latin tag, *Aut Deus aut homo non bonus*. Either Jesus was God, or he had no right to claim that he was God, and was therefore either insane or fraudulent. We find it abhorrent to assume that he was insane or fraudulent because of the depth and beauty of his character and teaching, and therefore we must conclude that he was God. This is the dilemma traditionally presented to the doubter. We can evade—indeed we must evade—this apparently stark dilemma by saying that Jesus did not claim to be God. At least, he did not claim to be God in the sense that would brand him as insane or fraudulent if his claim were not true. The dilemma presents a situation that never existed, and we can therefore confidently by-pass it.

Well, if we cannot prove our case by citing the words of Jesus himself, can we not at least claim that the early Church declared that Jesus was God Almighty, and can we not accept the early Church's claim as true? But even here we are not on very firm ground. Outside the first and twentieth chapters of the Fourth Gospel, no New

Testament writer says directly, explicitly, and clearly that Jesus is God. Of course they say a great many other things about him suggesting that he was superhuman or very closely associated with God, which we shall be considering in a moment, but for the most part they fight shy of describing him as God Almighty. They never describe him directly as divine (*theios*); even the Fourth Gospel does not use this word of Jesus. And some of the things that the New Testament writers say of Jesus suggest that they regard him as less than God Almighty. All through the book of Acts, for instance, Jesus is regarded as the instrument of God, but not as God himself, the man through whom God has acted, who has been raised from the dead, and who is now some sort of angelic being, but who certainly cannot be equated with God. It is difficult to read Revelation xv. 14–19 without concluding that somewhere in this passage Jesus Christ is being described as an angel. There is considerable support in the Christian literature of the end of the first and the beginning of the second centuries for the view that Christ was a kind of superior angel, and it may well be that Revelation supplies us with an instance of this belief. Again, we find in Paul a tendency to speak as if Jesus gained something by his incarnation. In Philippians ii. 5–11, for instance, he is given the Name that is above every name as a result of, as a reward for, his earthly career and sufferings. In 1 Corinthians xv. 20–28 Paul declares that Jesus shall reign until his kingdom is universally established; then he will hand it over to God and be subject to 'him who put all things under him'. And in the Epistle to the Hebrews it is written of him, 'In the days of his flesh, Jesus offered up prayers and supplications, with loud cries and tears, to him who was able to save him from death, and he was heard for his godly fear. Although he was a Son, he learnt obedience through what he suffered; and being made perfect he became the source of eternal salvation to all who obey him' (v. 7–9). Elsewhere the same work says that 'in that himself is able to suffer being tempted, he is able to succour them that are tempted' (ii. 18), as if Jesus learnt some new experience by the incarnation, and that 'we have not a high priest that cannot be touched with the feeling of our infirmities, but one that hath been in all points tempted like as we are, yet without sin' (iv. 15), which seems to suggest the same conclusion. Is this the language of men who regard Jesus Christ as in every way equal to God? Is it not much more like language used about some lesser, divine, or near-divine, being, but not about God Almighty? Perhaps we find ourselves driven to the conclusion that the New Testament is unorthodox. At any rate, surely after all this evidence we are left with no more than the ruins of a belief in the divinity of Jesus Christ. He did not claim to be God. If he had, his contemporaries would have rightly regarded him as insane. The early Church did not pretend that he was God Almighty, but only some lesser, semi-divine being. Why

should we today believe in his divinity? Why should we
not be content, as has already been suggested with some,
less equivocal but better-grounded position for him?
Surely we should be content with regarding him as the
supreme example of the sort of behaviour that we should
like to exhibit ourselves, or as a figure of outstanding
psychological penetration, as the great exponent of a
loving way of life, or as the teacher of great truths about
God, or some such simple and intelligible category that
can have a ready appeal to everybody in the twentieth
century? There does not seem to be any compelling
reason why we should regard Jesus as God, nor why we
should specially want to do so.

II

We shall now reverse the order of investigation that we
have so far followed, and instead of starting with the life
and words of Jesus and going on to the early Church's
interpretation of him we shall begin with the presentation of Jesus by the early Church and go on to look at his
life and words. The first fact to realize is the obvious and
now quite well-recognized but still important one, that
the New Testament presents Jesus in terms of Jewish
and not of Greek thought. Greek thought tends to be
static, to think of God in terms of status and quality and
essence. This is the type of thought used by the fourth-
century Church when it defined Jesus as of one substance

with the Father and as God of God, and it is the type of thought that has produced the very phrase 'the divinity of Jesus Christ'. But this is not the type of thought that the writers of the New Testament used, and if we put to the New Testament questions produced by this type of thought, such as 'Is Jesus of one substance with the Father?', it is not surprising that we receive confused and unsatisfactory answers. Jewish thought, on the other hand, is dynamic, conceiving of persons and things in terms of movement and of function rather than of status essence, and quality. Jewish thought is more interested in what God does than in what he is, in God as One who acts in history than in God as the Unmoved Mover or as the Absolute Being beyond all other being. And Jewish thought tends to think in images rather than in abstractions, in myth and parable and metaphor rather than in philosophy. It is highly characteristic of Jewish thought that it should present Jesus in eschatological terms, that is to say that it should present him in a framework of the world ending, of the old age going out and the new coming in, of final judgement and final salvation, of the kingdom of God and the Messianic time and the *parousia* and the age of the Spirit, among images of the heavens opening and the world passing away, of stars falling, the sun being darkened, and the moon turning to blood. For eschatological thought, that is thought set in the framework of the approaching end of the world, though it may strike us as bizarre and grotesque, is certainly

dynamic. It speaks of God acting and moving towards his
world, of the last reckoning and the last assize. In fact, if
we are to summarize what the New Testament writers
say of Jesus of Nazareth, we might fittingly say that they
think of him as the Last Act of God.

They do not, of course, all speak with the same voice.
In fact they present the significance of Jesus in a dozen
different and sometimes inconsistent patterns. In this
sense there is no theology of the New Testament, but
only a number of theologies. Mark presents him as the
Jesus with the Messianic secret, Matthew as the greater
than Moses, he who supersedes, perhaps he who in-
carnates, the Torah, the Law; Luke as the hope of the
Gentiles, able to reconcile Jew and Samaritan and pagan;
John as the incarnate Word of God full of grace and
truth. Paul has his own theology, the burning centre of
which is the Second Adam who was crucified in weakness
but lives in the power of God. The author of the Epistle
to the Hebrews sees Jesus as the great High Priest who
has done away with the old cult and the old sacrifice; the
author of the Revelation as the centre of history, round
whom revolve God's destiny and judgement for all races
and all nations. Many of these patterns themselves in-
corporate different, earlier, primitive patterns. The
writers of the New Testament almost vie with each other
in giving Jesus different titles and different functions. He
is the Son of Man, the Son of God, the Christ, the High
Priest, the New Israel, the Second Adam, the Man from

Heaven, the Servant of the Lord, the Righteous One, the Prophet foretold by Moses, the Lamb slain from the foundation of the world, the sacrificial offering, the Lion of Judah, the First-born of creation, the Image of God, the Word, the Bishop and Shepherd of our souls. They spread before us a dazzling variety of titles and functions drawn from the Old Testament, from Palestinian and from Hellenistic Judaism.

In all these titles they never—or hardly ever—describe him in static terms drawn from Aristotle, such as essence (*ousia*), nature (*physis*), or in terms of symbol-and-reality, temporary appearance contrasted with intellectual or inward truth, drawn from Plato. They think of Jesus in terms of function and of movement and of agency. They often describe him as executing a kind of parabola. He comes down from above, immerses himself in our life; plunges further down into death, rises again to our level at the resurrection, and at the Ascension returns to infinity. They describe again and again not what he is but what he *does*. He reconciles, he breaks down the barrier, he approaches God on our behalf, he atones, he takes our sins on himself, he gives his life or himself for us, he gives us life, he cleanses and washes us, he is lifted up or offered or offers himself, he obeys, he suffers, he spills his blood for us, he speaks to us, he mediates, he removes the condemnation, he breaks the curse, overcomes the law, draws the sting of death, manifests his glory and God's, enters heaven. Above all, he conquers. He is the great Victor, the great Doer, the great Accomplisher. This mode of expressing itself in terms of movement and function of New Testament Christology explains the apparent readiness of the authors to subordinate Jesus Christ to God the Father, to regard him as not quite equal to the Father. It is the Jewish way of explaining that the career of Jesus is the Act of God. The authors are describing a drama, which means a doing. It is no accident that modern drama arose out of the medieval mystery-play, for the mystery-play was describing a story that is essentially dramatic. This mixing of the Son of God with us, this assumption of solidarity with us on the part of Jesus Christ, this going down into death for us and with us, and rising again and returning to his former status with something done, something achieved, something rescued—all this can only be described in terms of movement out from God and back to God, so that the agent and mover brings back to God what he came to gain. Only thus can God be committed into and engaged with our life and our history, only thus can the act be really God's act. In their anxiety to describe this act as God's, the writers of the New Testament are not usually concerned to work out a consistent status for Jesus in relation to God. In their concern for what he does, or rather for what God does through him, they do not bother very much about what he is.

There are, of course, statements about the significance of Jesus in the New Testament that are not dynamic and functional, and they are impressive enough. The Fourth Gospel says 'The Word was God'. The Epistle to the Colossians calls him 'the image of the invisible God', and says that in him all the fulness of God was pleased to dwell (i. 15, 19). 1 Corinthians says that Christ has the mind of God (ii. 16), and Philippians that he was originally in the form of God (ii. 6), and the Epistle to the Hebrews that he reflects the glory of God and bears the very stamp of his nature (i. 3). The very fact that all these statements are different is impressive. Different writers testify in a number of diverse ways to the closeness of Christ to God. Their language is not that of the Nicene Creed, but it could be said to be on the way to it.

The patterns of interpretation, then, applied to Jesus by the writers of the New Testament vary widely, and contain several different traditions and sources. But they all exhibit certain common features. They all are descriptions of the risen Jesus, of Jesus as Lord, the Jesus of the Church's faith and preaching, Jesus of the time before and after his earthly career as well as during it, Jesus who is the communication from God, and not Jesus simply as a figure of worldly history, nor primarily as a rabbi, or a genius, or a saint, or a martyr, or a teacher. They none of them, however, are purely mythical or speculative accounts of Jesus, for they all involve the fact that he was crucified. Even the most apparently far-fetched and exotic account of him, such as that of the book of Revelation, has to accommodate itself to this brute fact, this grim piece of history. And they all, from first to last, whether early or late, whether Palestinian or Hellenistic, they all are eschatological.

This last point cannot be emphasized too often, for it is the most significant of all. We have noticed that Jewish thinkers do not express their concepts of God in terms of status, essence, or quality, but in dynamic terms and terms suggesting movement. Eschatology is the most dynamic mode of thought of all, and the whole New Testament is soaked in eschatology, from the point where Matthew in his genealogy places Jesus at the end of Israel's history to the point where Revelation places him at the end of the world's time. This is the meaning of the kingdom of God in the Synoptic Gospels. This is the keynote to the thought of St. Paul. This lies behind the fine writing and curious exegesis of Hebrews, in spite of its alleged Platonic leanings. Even John, in his own peculiar and profound Johannine way, has a kind of sublimated eschatology. Jesus Christ is the Last Man, God's Last Word and Last Act. With him has come final salvation and final judgement. With him has come the Holy Spirit, who is no mere pale understudy to Jesus, but God-at-the-end-of-the-world, God ruling among his redeemed people at the last time, heaven-in-himself, foretaste of final salvation; the surest sign of all that the ends of the ages are come upon us. Now that Jesus has risen the New Order is here; the Church stands between the Cross and the End. His coming is so important that the only really important thing that can happen after it is the end of the world. If we ask the New Testament what sort of significance has Jesus, it does not reply, in a philosophical, Aristotelian way, that he is the second *hypostasis* in a *trias*, of one substance with the Father as touching his Godhead. But it does say, in its Jewish eschatological way, that his significance is unlimited. He is of literally the last importance, for he is God's last Word and last Act. In its own way, the New Testament appears to be saying much the same thing as the Nicene Creed says in its very different way.

III

But we must ask, however briefly, one more question and answer it, however sketchily. What did Jesus say of himself? If he did not claim to be God, was not all this development or divinization that took place afterwards a vast mistake? Would it not be better to abandon the edifice of theology that seems to have been built so spectacularly and in such a short time upon the life of Jesus? Would it not be better to go back—if we want to go anywhere in this matter—to some simpler, more human and appealing, more historical, perhaps more realistic, account of Jesus?

Jesus certainly never said 'I am God', without qualification. But then, strange though it may seem, traditional orthodoxy has never held that Jesus did say this, or that he ever had any cause or right to do so. Even the strictest traditional orthodoxy has never held that Jesus Christ was God without qualification, that it would have been correct, for instance, after spending a day with Jesus in Capernaum, to say 'God went to sleep this afternoon' or 'God ate some fish this evening'. Still less has orthodoxy claimed that it is right and proper to say 'God died on the Cross', though in fact both the Christian father Tertullian and the modern novelist Dorothy Sayers did say so. Traditional Christian doctrine has always maintained that in the person of Jesus Christ the Word of God united a man with himself, or that the Word took human nature, never that in the incarnation either God turned into a man, as men turn into rabbits in fairy-tales, or that a man became God. So the bogey of a man walking the lanes of Galilee nearly two thousand years ago and saying 'I am God' should finally be laid. It is not even necessary to believe that Jesus was conscious that he was God; in fact the evidence seems to be distinctly against this view. It is true that our fathers would almost unanimously have claimed that he was conscious of his own divinity, but we have in the last hundred years become much more aware of the reality of the humanity of Jesus. We are able, not merely to assent intellectually to the proposition that he was man, as they did, but with the help of historical scholarship to imagine it more fully and vividly, and realize the limitations that this humanity implied.

And while we issue this warning against directly identifying Jesus of Nazareth with God from the side of ancient orthodoxy, we must issue another from the bosom of modern neo-orthodoxy. God, even as revealed in Jesus Christ, can only be known by faith. Could anyone have been able to say of Jesus Christ without qualification, 'There is God! Now we know what and where he is! There need be no more doubt', then this would have been idolatry and not response to revelation. The New Testament is aware of this, and preserves carefully what has been called the 'relativism' of faith. It is only Christ after the resurrection who is hailed as God by Thomas in the Fourth Gospel (John xx. 28). In this life we walk by faith, not by sight, even in the instance of recognizing God in Jesus Christ. We do not enjoy the unmodified certainties of heaven. Even the disciples in Galilee could not have indulged in a God-spotting expedition. We must approach God in fear and trembling, with faith and humility, or we miss him. This was as true for the contemporaries of Jesus in the last century as it is for us in the twentieth.

Again, in the recognition of God in Jesus Christ there must be the possibility of offence and of scandal. If intellectuals in the twentieth century want a concept of the significance of Jesus Christ that can easily be accepted as scientific or readily identified as an historical fact, or even understood as demanding a purely intellectual assent, it is the duty of the Church to disappoint them.

God demands faith from us, and such a demand involves
the possibility of unfaith and rejection. Faith is not a
mere believing of six impossible things before breakfast
(in the words of *Alice Through the Looking Glass*), but it
is a moral act; it entails commitment, it is something
disturbing and exacting. Faith in God as speaking to us
in Jesus Christ is no exception to this rule. We must not
smoothly equate this faith with general judgements
about history and culture.

As we try to determine what Jesus thought about himself we are unable to reconstruct with confidence the
categories of thought that Jesus employed to explain his
significance and his mission. The business of spotting
these has long become the work of experts, and the
experts, at the present stage of the development of Form
Criticism, are in a state of deplorable but unavoidable
confusion. The whole gamut of possibilities has been
explored—Son of Man, Son of God, Messiah, figure
from the Similitudes of Enoch or a Saviour from the
musings of the Gnostics, and so on. Scholarship cannot
give us any clear light as to which of these derive from the
interpretative patterns of the early Church and which, if
any, were used by Jesus himself. But we can detect an
eschatological note in his teaching corresponding to the
eschatological note in the Church's teaching about him.
It is impossible to remove the concept of the kingdom of
God from the teaching of Jesus (though a few heroic
souls have tried to do so), and the kingdom of God is a

wholly eschatological image. He did claim that the last time had come with him or round him, and that he was authorized by God to preach the Gospel of the last time. The insight of the late Albert Schweitzer that eschatology is the key to the understanding of the message of Jesus about himself remains a permanent contribution to the understanding of Jesus. Plainly Jesus did in some form proclaim that with him the *eschaton*, the Last Act, had come. Schweitzer no doubt, in the first flush of his discovery, over-emphasized this fact and applied it too rigorously. But any subsequent attempts to remove the eschatological note from the teaching of Jesus have been quite unconvincing. The proclamation of the kingdom of God as the End, the last Act of God, is a focus that brings together coherently more of the teaching ascribed to Jesus than any other. It is quite consonant with the intellectual and religious atmosphere of first-century Judaism, and it accounts for the Church's eschatological interpretation of Jesus, which otherwise would be largely inexplicable. No doubt there are many other sides to the teaching of Jesus. No doubt there were many individual characteristic elements in it that we cannot and should not glibly account for by ascribing them to contemporary influences and sources. But that this teaching was given within a framework of eschatological urgency as a message from God of final importance, because delivered in the final Age, we cannot doubt.

Perhaps this is only one way of putting something else

more basic and more indelible still in the impression created by the historical Jesus. People when they met him did not of course say 'I met God walking by the lakeside yesterday'. But they did somehow find themselves faced through meeting him with the ultimate demand from God. Whether through parables and words addressed to crowds or through conversations or through healings, they found themselves called to faith. This was not just casual faith, but eschatological faith, faith in God as acting then and there towards them in urgent and ultimate demand. This faith was conditioned by its having been demanded through Jesus, through what he did and said and through the sort of man he was, through his power of self-giving and self-abandonment and through his openness to God. What, after all, made Paul and John and the author of Hebrews and the evangelist Luke associate Jesus with the love of God, as they all undeniably in different ways did? They must have seen in him some pattern of self-sacrifice, a strange refusal to please himself—to use Paul's own remarkable words from Rom. xv. 3—which shone out of his behaviour as a man of flesh and blood and above all out of his willingness to be crucified. If we are to regard the crucifixion as an unfortunate accident, not foreseen by Jesus, we shall be compelled to do violence to virtually all the evidence that we possess about his attitude to his death, not only to his words but to his acts in instituting the eucharist. It is no chance and no fantasy that caused the mind of the early

Church to see in Jesus's career and peculiarly in its end a power of unselfishness and indeed of self-abandonment that was fitted to form the centre of the patterns of thought that they wove about him. The words 'for us' (*huper hēmōn*) or 'for our sins' (*huper tōn hamartiōn hēmōn*) seem to me to be one of the most primitive elements in the Church's thought about Jesus. In estimating a man's character from his words and actions people of all ages may be mistaken about the man's intentions or ideas about himself. They may be inclined to exaggerate his self-confidence, his occult powers, even his holiness. But it is most unlikely that they will err in estimating his power to express love.

We see Jesus only from the other side of the crucifixion and resurrection, looking back at him in the days of his flesh through these events, so to speak. And these events were what made the Church put forward these far-reaching eschatological claims for him as the Act of God. Without the crucifixion and resurrection, the historical Jesus would be quite insignificant. That is why it is futile and short-sighted to say that we cannot believe in the divinity of Jesus Christ but we think that he was a very fine man, or an outstanding religious genius, or just a very good fellow, or that we accept the Christian ethic. Without the crucifixion and resurrection the character of Jesus would be unimportant and the Christian ethic not worth practising. But we cannot dispense with the historical Jesus, as some today would have us do. We must look

back at him as well as we can through the events of Good
Friday and of Easter, and as we look back to the time
before those events we preceive that there is a likeness of
lineament, a moving and touching continuity, between
the risen Lord as preached by the early Church and the
Jesus who walked the roads of Galilee and the streets of
Jerusalem. The resurrection alone, key event though it
was, does not entirely account for the outburst of eschatological interpretation that followed. It was not merely the
resurrection of Christ, but of *Jesus* Christ. And in that
Jesus we can see One who brought men and women face
to face with the ultimate demand from God.

IV

If finally we lift our eyes from the pages of the New
Testament and look instead at the long sweep of Christian
history, we shall perceive that the divinity of Jesus Christ
is not an expendable ingredient in Christianity. It is not
one of those things that can be dropped in the interests of
complying with modern thought. This is not to say that
all Christians everywhere have always had before their
eyes the exact words of the Nicene Creed or of the
Athanasian Creed. It is not to deny that the Church took a
long time—at least three centuries—to achieve the
formulation of those dogmas that define the divinity of
Jesus Christ. It must be freely admitted that many of the
statements about the significance of Christ by the Christian

writers in the early centuries are not consistent with the definitions of the later dogmas. But it was true from the very beginning and has been true ever since that Christ is the centre of the Christian religion, Christ as the concentration of God's activity towards men, Christ as the focal point of Christian prayer and of all Christian approach to God, Christ as the figure round whom all Christian thought and experience and activity moved. It is as true for any form of Christianity as it was for Paul's form that Christianity is Christ. This is as true for the most carefully-structured scholastic theology as it is for the crudest preaching of salvation among the sects of the Protestant underworld. But of course Christ is not the centre of Christian thought and life as a mere figure of history. It is not as a 'jolly good fellow', nor as a propagator of the Christian ethic, nor as an appealing figure who can be stripped of divinity but retained as a human person, that Christ has held this central place in Christian faith. It is because he has always been regarded as the revealer of God, as the image of the invisible God, as he who declares the God whom no man has seen at any time, that Christ has been the sustaining power and constant focus of Christianity.

Just because we are so familiar with the divinity of Christ, we tend to overlook it. But this doctrine is part of the fabric of our minds to a much greater extent than we usually realize. It is part of our tradition and in our blood. We are not for nothing the heirs of nineteen

hundred years of Christian thinking about Christ's
relationship to the Father. Our minds may reject the
traditional dogma, but we shall find it hard work to teach
our hearts to do so. Christ is of course a figure of history,
and we shall regret the day if we irresponsibly attempt to
detach him from history. But bound up with his historical
existence is his existence as Risen Lord and as Son of
God, and if we succeed in tearing the two apart we shall
find the Christian faith in ruins around us as a consequence.

This argument does not contend for an unbounded
reverence to be paid to the actual words of the dogmas in
which the Church defined the divinity of Jesus, for these
words were limited by the thought-forms and the philosophical assumptions of the age in which they were framed.
But the substance of what those words were trying to
express, the same phenomenon to which they were witnessing, is the very nerve-centre of Christianity, what has
just been called the centrality of Christ to all Christian
life and thought, prayer and activity, the concentration
of God on and in Christ. It was of this that the writers of
the New Testament were speaking in their many-sided
and diverse witness to him. This is what, in a very wide
variety of modes and forms, of formulae and cults and
traditions, Christians have always expressed, and what
they have known to be the meaning of Christianity. The
word 'divinity' itself is a transitory one, hastening no
doubt, as all words do in the end, towards obsolescence.

But Christ as the Life who has been given to us by God, and not invented or imagined by ourselves, is not transitory and is entirely contemporary. Christ as God is the heart that beats within the Christian Church and within the individual Christian's innermost being. We cannot and dare not ask that heart to stop beating.

3: The Resurrection of Christ

A. R. C. LEANEY

OUR difficulty in this instance is a simple one: it lies in being required to believe that an event occurred that is admittedly unique and involves a supernatural explanation, and for which there is not and cannot be any evidence by which we might as historians or as scientists prove it or refute it. We might sum up the difficulties of the ordinary man about this by saying, 'It is altogether too much to ask us to believe; you say it is a unique event, but why is the evidence not repeated? Why have appearances of the risen Christ ceased?'

Attack upon the Christian belief in the resurrection has most often been directed against the Gospel stories. In fact belief in the stories and belief in the resurrection are different things and we shall be concerned to show the distinction between the two. But it will be convenient to begin where the attack usually falls, that is with the Gospel stories. Opponents usually take one of two lines:

1. The disciples stole the body, and the appearances are their stories; they are therefore either conscious or unconscious lies, according to whether the teller of the story invented it or innocently repeated it.

2. Jesus was not quite dead, and revived. This fact was suppressed and his subsequent appearances gave rise to the belief that he had risen from the dead. As with the kind of attack, some of the disciples at least, on a theory of this kind, must have been party to a fraud.

These lines of attack must now be reviewed in turn: first, 'the disciples stole the body'. This explanation clearly regards the empty tomb as the main phenomenon to be explained, but this has never been regarded by itself as a proof of the resurrection. The New Testament as a whole lays the emphasis rather on the appearances: it is these that convinced the disciples. These appearances were clearly not the apparitions of a ghost, but events that convinced the disciples not only that Jesus was alive, but that he was alive in the sense of being possessed of eternal life. They were events whose purpose was to convince the witnesses not only that Jesus had risen from the dead, but also that he was endowed with authority to send them forth to preach the Gospel based on his being the lord of life. Indeed, the main event that happened to the disciples was this convincing and commissioning of them. Here the critic may intervene. Since the

conviction of the disciples and their obedience to the commission are facts of history, why not abandon the fairy-
tales of the Gospels and rely on this statement of the
matter? All we need say is this: the disciples became convinced that Jesus was not dead but alive and that he was
ordering them to proclaim a Gospel that included this
conviction. That they became convinced is the main
event. Is not this in fact the resurrection? This will prove
to be a fruitful line to pursue and we shall take it up
again later on. Before we follow it further we must consider the other line of attack, and even before this we
must make sure that we do not lose sight of the matter of
the empty tomb, because for some opponents it is this
that has to be explained away. The point to be made here
is that it seems that it had to be explained away relatively
early, before the first century was over; for Matthew in
his Gospel speaks of the common modern explanation as
if it were well established by the time he wrote. He
regards it as the 'official' Jewish explanation that the
disciples stole the body (Matt. xxviii. 13). We may in
passing note the surprising weakness of this explanation
without support from witnesses, specification of which
disciples, of the place of reburial, or of any challenge to
the early Christian claims based on this serious accusation.

We pass on to the second line of attack: 'Jesus was not
really dead and revived . . .'. We know from an incident
in the life of Josephus that it was possible to revive those
who had been crucified if they were taken down before

they died on the cross, but the chances against revival in such circumstances were very strong. Out of three of Josephus's friends removed from crosses and given the most careful attention only one survived (*Vita,* 75). If we consider the revival of Jesus as a serious possibility, we have to ask how much of the story we are prepared to accept: was he beaten, was he therefore exhausted before being crucified, was he pierced by a spear while on the Cross? *How* was he revived, how and by whom was he removed from the tomb, who gave him medical attention, where was he nursed back into health, what became of him afterwards, why do we hear nothing whatever about what he did afterwards? These questions are difficult to answer, but the type of critic whom we are considering is quite equal to them.

Joseph left the Praetorium, and with Nicodemus, who was impatiently awaiting him, hastened to Golgotha. There he received the body; he washed it, anointed it with spices, and laid it on a bed of moss in the rock-hewn grave. From the blood which was still flowing from the wound in the side, he ventured to draw a hopeful augury, and sent word to the Essene Brethren. They had a hold close by, and promised to watch over the body. In the first four-and-twenty hours no movement of life showed itself. Then came the earthquake. In the midst of the terrible commotion a Brother, in the white robes of the Order, was making his way to the grave by a secret path. When he, illumined by a flash of lightning, suddenly appeared above the grave, and at the same moment the earth shook violently, panic seized the watch, and they fled. In the morning the Brother hears a sound from the grave: Jesus is moving. The whole Order hastens to the spot, and Jesus is removed to their Lodge. Two brethren remain at the grave—these were the 'angels' whom the women saw later. Jesus, in the dress of a gardener, is afterwards recognized by Mary Magdalene. Later, He comes out at intervals from the hiding-place, where He is kept by the Brethren, and appears to the disciples. After forty days He took His leave of them: His strength was exhausted. The farewell scene gave rise to the mistaken impression of His Ascension.

This is an account by Schweitzer of a passage in a book originally written by Venturini in 1802. How modern it sounds with its Essenes, brought in without benefit of caves or Dead Sea! It is well worth quoting Schweitzer's own remark about this work:

Venturini's 'Non-supernatural History of the Great Prophet of Nazareth' may almost be said to be reissued annually down to the present day, for all the fictitious 'Lives' go back directly or indirectly to the type which he created. It is plagiarised more freely than any other Life of Jesus, although practically unknown by name.[1]

A further difficulty arises: if the critics we are considering are attacking belief in the appearances as untrue and based on false suppositions, then they must account for belief in the risen Christ. Their account of the matter is not adequate for this. Can an invalid who just

[1] *The Quest of the Historical Jesus*, pp. 46 f.

survived death by crucifixion and was known by those nearest to him so to have survived and subsequently to have died a natural death become the inspiration for a belief in the risen Lord as Christians have held it and died for it?

If on the other hand the critics are attacking belief in the risen Christ (which they are not aware of doing but one suspects may be the case), they have the still harder task of explaining why the Gospels were written at all.

Such approaches are far too uncritical and far too naïve. Such examination of the Gospel stories takes no account whatever of knowledge of the Gospels, or of their relation to one another and to tradition. To examine the evidence critically as far as it appears in the Gospels we must be much more thorough and one might say far less credulous. It is unnecessary to go into the details of Gospel criticism, and it is enough to state a position relevant to our problem. The first thing that must be said is that all the Gospels are written from the point of view of belief in the risen Christ, which means that he is regarded as Son of God. This tradition is early, as we can see from Rom. i. 4 where Jesus is clearly held to be Son of God because of the resurrection. The earliest Gospel, Mark, shows this conviction unmistakably, though it contains no account of the resurrection nor of any appearances, at least in the form of the Gospel as it has come down to us. Of the resurrection narratives in Luke and John we can

say both that they have much in common and that they
reveal a developed state of the tradition about the resurrection of Jesus. They share the basic story of an appearance in the Upper Room and of an appearance to Peter.
In the Fourth Gospel this appearance to Peter takes place
in Galilee; this is a curious circumstance, for Luke made
great efforts to give the impression that the apostles never
left Jerusalem but that all their work developed smoothly
from that of the Lord's. Apparently all this can now be
abandoned: to admit tacitly that there was a period when
the disciples retired to Galilee, and went fishing again, no
longer embarrasses. Indeed, the author adds to the story
about Peter the figure of doubtful historicity whose name
he refuses to give us, calling him only the Beloved
Disciple. In Luke the appearance to Peter takes place in
Galilee, indeed, but has been relegated to the Lord's
earthly ministry. It thus loses its character as a resurrection appearance, though it retains that of a commissioning (Luke v. 1–11). Two other stories more obviously
betray later development. These are the appearance to
Thomas and the walk to Emmaus. The former introduces
the element that those who hear the Gospel ought to
believe the witnesses; if they do so they are blessed,
believing even though unable to see the risen Lord for
themselves. The Emmaus story lays its emphasis on the
presence of the Lord at the eucharist. When we read
Matthew it is more than ever obvious that he is concerned among other things with a well-developed tradi-

tion, in his case that of Jewish adversaries, against which he defends the Christian tradition.

This Christian tradition, which lies behind all these treatments of it, whichever Gospel we consider, is not that of a story of the resurrection of Christ as an historical event. This is very clear if we take the well-developed form of it in the late Gospel, Matthew; the Lord's appearance to the women who have found the tomb empty is very short and shorn of all details. It is therefore striking to find emphasis given to the meeting in Galilee whither Jesus is to 'lead them forth' and so meet them there. The appearance to the disciples must take place in Galilee of the Gentiles, a place which in this Gospel alone is given specific prominence as the land where the people sit in darkness and light dawns on them (iv. 15 f.) Moreover, the meetingplace is 'the mountain' that Jesus had arranged as the place for it, the mountain presumably on which the Messiah had proclaimed the new Law and 'appeared' to them already at the Transfiguration. Jesus makes no attempt to overcome the doubts of some of the disciples but claims that he has received power over the whole world, and then sends them out. The tradition then is of a meeting of the Lord with his disciples for the purpose of commissioning them. No doubt conviction that he is alive is implied, but it is included in the other and primary task.

A glance at the other Gospels will confirm this impression: Luke is concerned to bring the disciples' task within their reach by arming them with conviction and with power to convince others through understanding of the Scriptures. The death of the Messiah had been foreseen. This will be no stumbling-block for the preacher who is equipped for his task. Stay in Jerusalem, await power, then preach the Gospel. Within this account of commissioning is narrated a striking and unforgettable story of an appearance in the upper room whose purpose is indeed to convince the disciples that the Lord is alive; but this is not the only purpose of his coming to them. To this also is joined the act of commissioning: Jesus tells them to await the power to discharge their task, and then discharge it; it is not simply to proclaim to the world that he has risen, though no doubt that is a necessary part of it. They are to proclaim the gospel of the forgiveness of sins to all nations. This is indeed to preach the risen Lord.

The Fourth Gospel seems to share with Luke this tradition of an appearance in the upper room, and tells the famous story of Thomas in order to add a message to readers far removed in time from the events that he narrates: they are to believe the witnesses. Here again we find what we found in Luke, the emphasis on convincing that the Lord is alive, and the commissioning, in this Gospel with a different way of bestowing the necessary power to carry out the task for which they are commissioned. Then the Fourth Gospel adds the story about the appearance in Galilee which is in effect a commissioning of Peter of a rather ceremonial kind. It should be noted that in this story there is no element of conveying the fact that he who died has risen. That he is the risen Christ is taken for granted: the chapter (John xxi) begins by making this quite clear: 'After this Jesus manifested himself again . . .'.

We venture to conclude that the tradition in these stories is a commissioning of disciples hitherto unfit for their task through a sense of defeat and despair. Thus the commissioning by the Lord must not only be by the living Lord (John xxi) but also by one who is seen and acknowledged to be the living Lord by those who are commissioned. Such a statement seems necessary, to preserve the balance of what is taught by these elements in the Gospels.

At this point a question seems to arise from the critical point of view that we have taken. We have held that there is a persistent tradition behind the appearance stories in the Gospels, but that these latter are various, and exhibit clear signs of having been developed from an original core. Is this original core then not a public event but a conviction in the minds of the earliest missionaries, the apostles and their helpers? It seems clear that the risen Christ did convince and commission his disciples. But are not the descriptions of *how* he did this too naïve and too bound to the thought of the time to be of any value as historical evidence? Do not these stories *represent* a truth which in itself must not be identified with any of these ways of putting that truth? And can we

not formulate that truth quite clearly to ourselves without
recourse to any of these stories? If we attempt to do so,
we shall say something like this: the Lord who died on
the Cross was really the Lord of the universe. His death
was a conquest of the evil powers and the power that he
embodied in this task is available to all who will accept the
crucified Lord's power for themselves, enabling them to
live liberated from their old sinful selves, to live hence-
forth under the power and *by* the power of God. We
cannot proclaim this unless we believe we are proclaiming
a living Lord who was crucified. To those who proclaim,
then, he is a—or rather, the—living Lord and it is His
Word that is proclaimed. It is proclaimed with power,
and this causes it to be accepted as a word of power. Thus
not only those who proclaim but those who accept are
witnessing to the power of the Word which is the resurrection of Christ, the resurrection for and in all who
believe and accept and trust. Thus history is understood
in another sense from the mere record of facts that
'actually happened'. We are not to inquire whether
something happened but decide for ourselves that the
crucified is for us and we are for him. If we think we can
make our decision attend upon a previous decision that
some event occurred in history (understood as the record
of what actually happened), then we make the Gospel of
God depend upon a human inquiry.

The truth in this point of view is manifest. At least
part of it may be put like this: to accept the Gospel does

not involve simply an assent to the statement that Jesus rose from the grave on the third day. Such an assent would be possible without faith. To accept the Gospel involves trust in the risen Christ, the living one. In other words, we are called on to believe in Christ, not the resurrection.

For any view of this kind, associated usually with the name of Bultmann, the historical Jesus is irrelevant, and Paul's insistence upon this may be quoted in support. We are not to know Christ after the flesh (2 Cor. v. 16). Bultmann's followers, Fuchs, Bornkamm, Käsemann, J. M. Robinson, have modified this attitude to the extent of arguing for the relevance of what may be stated about the historical Jesus; but their modification does not extend to regarding the resurrection as an historical event in the sense of an event occurring within the restrictions of time and place and in principle publicly verifiable. For them, as for Bultmann, the resurrection stories are unauthentic —legends that are the results of the resurrection, not a foundation for belief in it.

In order to reach a statement that will do justice to this view without doing violence to the evidence of the Gospels, let us turn to a brief inspection of the case of Paul. As we carry this out, we shall leave on one side the contribution of Acts, on the ground that this book tells stories about his conversion that cannot be shown to be authentic and can be shown to carry the encrustation of interpretation; indeed, many would hold them to be altogether legendary. If they are legends, they have an historical core, and this can be recovered from Paul's own writings. From these we can derive the following points relevant to our subject: the first is that according to Paul himself some event occurred and it was God who acted to bring this event about for the purpose of converting Paul and commissioning him. On this, insisting on the divine initiative, Paul based his authority.

The second point is that Paul is reticent as to details. He speaks firmly and clearly about the time 'when he, who from my mother's womb set me apart and called me through his grace, thought well to reveal his son in me' (Gal. i. 15 f.) and claims to have seen the Lord in a context that seems to imply the risen Lord (1 Cor. ix. 1). If we attend to these two points alone we might be tempted to conclude that Paul provides good evidence for saying that the essence of a resurrection experience was quite private and 'inner', and not an appearance that could be verified by any other person.

The third point is that Paul forbids this conclusion by calling the event an appearance, and, most important, the last that the Lord made in a series of appearances whose significance lies in the fact that they make belief in a purely 'spiritual' resurrection impossible (1 Cor. xv. 3–8). Paul's motive in introducing this passage is often discussed and our decision upon this depends upon the conclusion reached about the situation between him and his Corinthian converts at the time; but whether it is to prove that there is such a thing as resurrection, or to prove that there is a resurrection of the *body*, or that Christ rose from the dead, the reiteration of 'he appeared' in this famous passage makes it quite clear that he is repeating a firmly-held early tradition of the Church that a number of people *saw* the risen Christ.

The conclusion seems inescapable: it is no doubt true that for Paul, as for all previous and subsequent Christians, faith has been in the risen Christ and not in the mere fact of the resurrection. But examination of different types of evidence suggests that in the experience of those who founded the Church their being convinced, and their acceptance of the commission to proclaim this conviction, at least included (we need not necessarily say involved) having demonstrated to them that he was the risen Lord, not an apparition—not dead, but 'I myself'— the Jesus of the earthly ministry whom they had known 'after the flesh'. To concede that the stories in the Gospels may owe so much to doctrine as to conceal rather than to reveal 'what actually happened' is not to concede that they are altogether legendary.

Many questions remain, and only a few can be mentioned: for example, is the empty tomb fact or legend? According to the view expressed here it might seem to be a matter of indifference, but it has in fact a definite relevance in connection with a vital point in the Gospel presentation—the insistence on the continuity between the risen Lord and the Jesus known in Galilee. On this

point the followers of Bultmann seem nearer a just
account of the matter than Bultmann himself, for it is
vital to see that this connection is preserved in the Gospel.
If it was not Jesus who rose and appeared to the disciples,
then it was someone bearing a very mysterious relation
to him, a relation impossible to explain. If it was Jesus,
it follows that the tomb would be empty.

A further question was mentioned at the beginning:
why have appearances ceased? To answer this adequately
the Ascension and Exaltation of the Lord to his throne
at the right hand of God would need to be expounded and
perhaps re-expressed in un-biblical contemporary terms,
for these are ideas alien to our minds, which yet hold a
vital truth. According to the New Testament the Lord has
passed from this earth to heaven. An attempt at re-
expressing this might say that he has passed out of our
physical sphere into another dimension. To resume
Biblical language, he is present at the eucharist though
essentially in heaven. He is perhaps also present in a
certain way by speaking to us through our study of the
Scriptures. He is present by his Spirit. Thus, Christ
dwells in the eternal sphere but his manner of communication with us is faithful to the principle of the incarnation, that the eternal enters within the temporal even
under the conditions of the temporal; he comes to us
therefore in sacramental ways. We are not required to
know him otherwise and directly in this our mutual
order of being ('after the flesh'). But there were time

and place when and where this was possible, and this is part of history in a quite usual sense of the word. If the incarnation expresses the Lord's entering into history, his resurrection and Ascension express his liberation from its restrictions. In whatever sense we regard them as historical, or unhistorical, they express his relation to us, and upon that our salvation depends.

4: God and Guilt

H. McKEATING

IN this study I shall endeavour to show that:

1. The problem of guilt is a real problem, i.e. it is a problem not only for those who take a religious view of life. It is a problem not manufactured by Christians, though Christians differ from most non-Christians in the significance that they attach to it.

2. The Christian's answer to the problem of guilt (an answer that he finds in the work of Christ) can only be expressed completely in what may broadly be called 'mythological' terms (e.g. in terms of sacrifice offered to God, of victory over the devil, of redemption or ransom from sin, etc.).

3. Though the Christian answer cannot be completely given in non-mythological terms, nevertheless some sort of answer in non-mythological terms must be attempted.

4. I shall offer what seem to me some possible lines on which such an attempt might be made. In doing this I

shall explore the nature of the connection between the life and death of Jesus of Nazareth and ourselves, now.

I

Guilt is a fact. That is to say, all human beings at one time or another are subject to guilt *feelings*. We usually feel guilty when we have offended against standards of conduct that we accept as normative, whether those standards are set by our society at large, by a sub-society to which we belong (such as the Church), or whether they are standards that we have selected for ourselves.

But guilt feelings are neither as simple nor as rational as they appear at first sight. Feelings that are psychologically indistinguishable from those caused by genuine, rationally recognized moral lapses are also caused in some of us by circumstances of other kinds. Guilt feelings may arise because the conscience lags behind a developing moral consciousness. I have been brought up, let us say, to believe that certain actions are wrong. I come, on mature reflection, to the conviction that they are not wrong at all. Nevertheless, if I indulge in them, the same guilt feelings arise as formerly. The conscience is here out of step with the rational moral judgement.

Even more irrationally, a person (a normal person) may have powerful feelings of guilt caused by a situation for which he and everybody else would recognize that he is not responsible. A child may have acute guilt feelings about his parents' quarrels. An individual may feel guilty because he knows himself to be illegitimate. Examples of this kind of irrational guilt feeling could be multiplied.

But are feelings of this irrational kind theologically relevant? Does irrational guilt, do mere feelings of guilt, matter? To most religious men throughout human history it has seemed that they do. A large part of the business of religion has always been concerned with the expiation of guilt, and often with precisely that part of guilt that could not be attributed to the commission of particular offences against particular laws, but a guilt, nevertheless, of which man is from time to time uneasily and even overpoweringly aware.

Much of the guilt of which ancient man was conscious we would be inclined to set down as superstitious, rather than religious in our sense of the word. Not infrequently, odd though it may seem to us, ancient man was convinced that he had offended and must make expiation, but knew neither how he had offended or against what or whom the offence had been committed. Even odder, to our mind, is the fact that he did not always consider it important to find out.

Are we to be guided, though, by the feelings and convictions of ancient, not to say primitive, men? Not precisely. I cite these examples in order to illustrate my belief that guilt is a fact of human existence and is deeply rooted in the human psyche; that in both its rational and irrational manifestations it raises real problems and has always done so; and that it has traditionally been the job of religion to deal with both its rational and irrational manifestations.

Of course, there are perfectly good biological reasons for the existence of the phenomenon of guilt feelings. It can be argued that it is biologically necessary for a social organism such as man to develop the capacity to feel guilt, for guilt feelings (the conscience, if you like) are what warns an individual when he steps out of line with the rest of his community, when he lets his community down. Man could not survive except as a social animal. He could not survive unless the individual could be induced generally to put the group before self. Primitive man could not afford the luxury of non-conformity. In unity alone lay strength and survival. The conscience is the mechanism that ensures this conformity and unity.

In modern man the conscience may be less necessary, though we could not, socially speaking, dispense with it altogether. We suffer from its survival into an age in which it has become partly redundant. Or perhaps we could say that we suffer from the fact that the conscience is still excited by stimuli that were relevant in some evolutionarily earlier stage of human development but are irrelevant now.

If one is looking for a biological or psychological explanation, I suppose that one along these lines might be held to be reasonably adequate, though I would point out that it does not explain why the conscience occasionally impels a man not to conform to his community's standards but to criticize them. What the Christian would dispute is not whether a biological explanation of the origin of guilt feelings is true, but whether it is sufficient. Even if such an explanation is true as far as it goes, it does not therefore follow that the mere recognition of the origin of irrational feelings of guilt will be sufficient to cause them to disappear. It does not follow that the fact of human guilt tells us nothing of significance about human nature.

Guilt feelings persist. Not all of them are felt on reflection to be irrational. They attach themselves most frequently to acts or omissions that most of us would recognize to be real moral offences, and the conviction of guilt is as much a problem to contemporary man as it was to ancient or primitive man.

Not only Christians have consciences. This may seem an obvious fact, but there are contexts in which Christians infuriate non-Christians by appearing to forget it. Christians talk glibly about the decline of moral standards, and choose to ignore tha fact that in our day almost all public issues are discussed in rather anxious moral terms.

I take two examples, quite at random. As I write this, my morning paper carries two front-page headlines. On the left of the page, Rhodesia (again); on the right, road accidents in fog on motorways. Rarely in all these weeks (or is it months?) that the Rhodesia crisis has been with us have I seen any discussion of the matter that had much to say about the balance of economic or political advantage to Britain of the various possible courses of action. When such questions have been raised, they have always been made to sound like secondary considerations. What I have been bombarded with are discussions of the balance of moral responsibilities. How do we balance our moral responsibility for the black Africans of Rhodesia with our undoubted responsibility for the white ones?

As to the road accidents, it is always our consciences that are appealed to in discussions of this issue. As far as the particular topic of the motorway accidents in fog is concerned, this is especially clear. Everybody is unanimous in ascribing them to criminal irresponsibility.

Leaving these two issues aside, we live in an age of protest, of protest marches, protest literature, protest songs. And all these protests are moral protests. The making of moral protests has become a national sport, and not only in our own nation. Whether it is the war in Vietnam that excites us, the ubiquitous race question, or merely blood sports, we all wear our consciences on our sleeves.

There is one rather striking fact to be noticed about every public issue I have named: in no case is our responsibility for the state of affairs we object to a purely individual responsibility. In some cases it is not a direct responsibility at all. I had no direct part in determining the Government's attitude to the Vietnam war; I have never taken part in a race riot; I have never been involved in a road accident or hunted a fox in my life. Most Englishmen could say the same. Yet we are told, and are inclined to accept the fact, that we have a moral responsibility in all these matters. It is our society as a whole that is responsible. We are collectively responsible, corporately guilty.

The textbooks on theology that I read tell me that ancient men, the kind of men who wrote the Bible, thought in communal terms. They thought in terms of communal responsibility and of corporate guilt. Ancient man, they suggest, though they do not say so in so many words, was distinctly odd, and a good deal of our difficulty with his ideas is that we ourselves think in terms that are unrepentantly individualistic.

I suggest that the textbooks on theology are wrong about this. I suggest that the popular mind, whether in ancient or in modern times, finds the ideas of corporate moral responsibility and corporate guilt meaningful. I do not mean that the ideas of corporate responsibility that the Biblical writers assumed are necessarily identical with our own. They are not. But there are points of contact. And I suggest that this is one of the difficulties for Christian belief that we ought not to find insuperable.

If we turn from the organs of public opinion and look at our contemporary serious literature we find some of these same conclusions borne out. Not a few of our contemporary writers are concerned about questions of morality and guilt. Again, I might add that the Church, by and large, has not noticed this. It notes that very many of our contemporary writers are not over-concerned about sexual morality, and therefore dismisses them as rather nasty. We may properly regret the lack of concern over sexual morality. Sexual morality is important. But to conclude that because some of our non-Christian contemporaries ignore this issue they are not bothered about morality at all is to display merely the narrowness of our own terms of reference.

There is not time for a multitude of examples, but one species of writing that provides them in some number is the one we might broadly call social novels and stories. Over the last fifteen years or so in this country we have seen quite a spate of these, most of them taking as their background the English class system and many of them making quite serious judgements, moral judgements, upon it.

A not altogether typical but very popular example is John Braine's novel *Room at the Top*. This is a very entertaining work of fiction, but it is also a serious presentation of the issues raised in one man's mind by his deliberate progress from one social stratum to another. It analyses the tension roused in his personality and his perception of what he feels to be the sacrifices of moral principle involved in his progress. It weighs the relative

values of social ambition against some of the more re-
warding aspects of human relationships, and records the
struggle involved as the hero sacrifices the one for the
other. The book's closing lines leave us in no doubt that
what we have been reading is, among other things, a
study in guilt.

I doubt whether Mr. Braine, or many of the
other writers whom I have unfairly lumped together as
writers of social novels, would call themselves Christians.
Most of them certainly do not write as if they had any
Christian axe to grind. Yet a profound moral awareness
underlies a good deal of their work.

I think that if we turned to America, a society that is
far more acutely self-critical than is our own, we could
find an embarrassment of examples of works of literature
whose principal aim, or one of whose aims, is to offer a
moral criticism of their society. The works of William
Faulkner, John Steinbeck, and Arthur Miller are examples that spring readily to my mind, out of my very
inadequate reading in this field.

In our day the writer has taken over the role of prophet. He considers it his duty to probe our complacency,
to expose us to our responsibilities. His message is very
often that if we do not feel guilty then we certainly ought
to do so. We have so much to feel guilty about.

The most striking instance of all in my own limited
literary knowledge is that of the French writer, Albert
Camus. M. Camus was an avowed atheist. Yet in his

novel *The Fall*, if I have properly grasped it, he is saying that if we are to understand what man is (if indeed we are to understand ourselves) we must see him first of all as guilty. And this fact, the fact of his guilt, is the most significant thing about him.

Guilt, then, is a fact. Some guilt feelings are irrational, or apparently so. Some guilt feelings spring from superstition rather than morality. But many guilt feelings are caused by our rational conviction of moral failure. This guilt and moral failure are taken seriously by many people who are not Christians. Indeed, if they were not taken seriously it is doubtful whether society could in the long run survive.

The Christian nevertheless differs from most non-Christians in the kind of importance he attaches to feelings of guilt. He not only refuses to write them off as a kind of evolutionary hangover, but he also refuses to see them as of merely social significance. He asserts that there is a transcendent basis for morality. All moral offences are committed ultimately against a moral order whose basis and justification are not in society itself but beyond it. They are committed against God.

Furthermore, the Christian is convinced that guilt and moral failure are not merely accidental; not something that might be avoided, given a little more goodwill, a little more moral effort. Guilt is endemic. Man is born to failure as the sparks fly upwards.

The Christian is compelled to this conclusion by his

own experience of moral effort, by his observation of the
world, and by the corporate experience and observation
of the Church. While neither ignorant nor unappre-
ciative of the moral and spiritual successes of determined
men, he finds everywhere evidence of the ultimate
ineffectiveness of human idealism.

All this is enshrined in the traditional Christian doctrine of original sin. The doctrine of original sin is perhaps the most widely misunderstood of all Christian
doctrines. It is believed by some, even inside the Church,
that it has been universally abandoned, because it is such
obvious nonsense.

Some ill-informed people, such as those who write
articles for the *Observer*, seem to think that it has something to do with sex. One young lady propounded in its
columns a short while ago the theory that the doctrine of
original sin was invented by the theologians, in the days
when people actually used to listen to theologians, to
discourage them from indulging their impulses in a
healthy, natural (that is to say, thoroughly promiscuous)
fashion.

The doctrine of original sin is certainly open to misunderstanding, and therefore has to be stated especially
carefully. Some of the ways of stating it that satisfied
Christians in the past make a disagreeable impression on
many of us today.

But however we state the doctrine, our statement must
convey these convictions: (*a*) Moral failure is endemic.

No man can avoid it: First, because he does not always perceive what is right. Second, because when he perceives what is right he does not always have the strength of character to pursue it. Third, because when he does pursue what is right he does not consistently succeed in achieving the good that he sees. (*b*) There is something that may rightly be called corporate sin and corporate guilt, i.e. that there is a guilt I bear that is something more than the sum total of blame for all the offences that I, individually, have committed. (*c*) This guilt of mine creates its own kind of vicious circle, in which the legacy of failure is failure, and in which today's lapse renders me less capable of facing tomorrow's test.

II

The Christian finds the answer to the problems of guilt and sin in the work of Christ. The work of Christ includes his incarnation, his life among us, his death and resurrection, his Ascension, his sending to us of his Holy Spirit, and his coming in glory.

Now this work is interpreted by the New Testament writers, and has been interpreted by most Christian thinkers since, in almost exclusively mythological terms. We are told that Christ is the 'New Adam', who by his obedience undoes the results of the disobedience of the first Adam and is able to generate a new race of mankind, a new creation. We are told that on our behalf Christ

fought a battle with the evil powers who held us captive
in sin and death, and that having defeated them he has
freed us from them for ever. We are told that by the
sacrifice of his life Christ has appeased the just wrath of
God against us, or that he has accepted in his own person the punishments that ought rightly to have been
ours.

This is by no means an exhaustive list of the explanations that have been offered of the way in which the
work of Christ has its effect on us, but it is sufficient to
indicate the general nature of most of the theories.

This point, the point at which he is required to explain
or set out the doctrine of the Atonement, is the one where
the Christian finds it most difficult to avoid traditional
imagery and mythological statements.

For example, Dr. Alec Vidler, in his *Plain Man's
Guide to Christianity*, when he comes to his exposition
of the Atonement, simply asserts the primacy of sacrificial language both in the Bible and in the traditions and
the liturgy of the Church, and he flatly refuses, plain
man or no plain man, to translate it into any other.

On a very different level, we may look at that modern
parable by William Golding, *Lord of the Flies*. This is a
remarkable literary and theological *tour de force*, but
one's immediate criticism of it is that it moves too uneasily on too many different levels. His little boys cast
away on a desert island recapitulate the history of the
race. The exposition of original sin is impressive and

convincing. And the sin is real sin. It ends with real murder, real torture, and real, literal idolatry. But as soon as we move to atonement we enter immediately the realm of the figurative. In real terms the saviour-figure accomplishes practically nothing. He removes the corpse of a dead airman, which certainly is one of the elements that the boys' imagination has magnified into the Beast. But what else does he do? The sin is real, its removal is no more than symbolic.

These examples illustrate our dilemma. Guilt and moral failure are real enough. Yet when we speak of the answer to them we fall back on what is to most of us the unsatisfactory language of metaphor or myth.

Moreover, the metaphors or myths in terms of which the traditional theories are stated are to most twentieth-century minds strange, meaningless, or repellent. They often appear to imply a doctrine of God and an understanding of his character that is unacceptable to us. Perhaps this is partly our own fault. Perhaps we often read into the traditional images ideas that we were never meant to see there. But to say this does not remove our difficulty.

As an illustration of our difficulties we may consider the imagery of sacrifice. The concept of sacrifice was one that the New Testament writers and later thinkers all found very useful. It enters in one way or another into very nearly all of the traditional theories of the Atonement. It is not untrue to say that for Christians of earlier ages the idea of sacrifice was the key to the whole problem of the interpretation of the work of Christ.

In Biblical times everyone was familiar with sacrifice as an institution, Jew and pagan alike. They were familiar with the idea that a gift brought to the altar, or the blood of an animal poured out beside it, or flesh burnt on it, or the meat of an animal eaten in the sanctuary, was somehow pleasing to God. They assumed that such performances disposed God favourably to one's prayers and made one's person acceptable to him, and procured at once an expiation of guilt and a renewal of life and health.

But how was the sacrifice supposed to achieve its effect? Much scholarly ink has flowed in the discussion of this question. Theories of sacrifice have been propounded, defended, and demolished. There is evidence for and against almost any theory one cares to conceive. But no definitive answer is ever likely to be given to the question. The reason is not far to seek. Ancient man himself had no theory of sacrifice. Or at least he had no consistent theory. He did not in the normal way feel the need of one. Sacrifice was an institution he had accepted from his forefathers. It had an impressive history. It was not for him to inquire how it worked. It was sufficient that it did, and the fact that it did he would probably have regarded as a matter of observation.

Now for us, none of this is true. We are not familiar with sacrifice as an institution. If we were to accept it we should certainly feel the need of a theory to explain how it worked. And no conceivable theory could be congenial to any understanding of the nature of God that we would find satisfying. What to most Christians throughout the Church's history has been an *explanation* of the Atonement is to us something that needs *to be explained*.

The New Testament and Christian tradition insist on expounding the meaning of the work of Christ in mythological terms and images, and they happen for the most part to be terms and images that fail to catch the imagination of modern western man.

III

Nevertheless, other attempts have been made to express an understanding of the work of Christ, and attempts that perhaps strain the credulity less. Of these others the one that has been historically the most important is undoubtedly that of Abelard. Abelard was a monk of the eleventh and twelfth centuries whose life-story is a romance. A knowlege of this romance is very helpful to a sympathetic understanding of his theology, but for our present purposes we must dispense with an account of it.[1] Abelard did use the conventional and traditional explanations, but his own original contribution was a radically

[1] The story is told remarkably well by Miss Helen Waddell in her historical novel *Peter Abelard*.

new departure. Abelard sees the work of Christ principally as a demonstration of the love of God, and this
demonstration saves us from our sins because when we
behold it we are moved to love. Moved by love we become open to God, we give up our sins.

Many theories have followed that of Abelard, all
sharing the same essential characteristic, that they move
the focus of attention from what God in Christ does *for us*
to what God in Christ does *in us*.

What I have called the mythological theories all have
one thing in common; they speak as if the work of Christ
effected either a change in the attitude of God or a change
in the power over us of evil forces. Abelard's theory
speaks of a change in the attitude of man. God remains
the same, and the work of Christ does not alter his attitude at all. It demonstrates rather what his attitude is
all the time. The potency of the evil powers remains, in
itself, the same. What changes is man's perception of the
situation and his response to it.

Now as long as we speak in mythological terms we are
able to preserve the idea that the work of Christ accomplishes something objective; the idea that something has
been done that is independent of our attitude to it; that
something would still have been done whether we
responded to it or not, whether we believed in it or not.
Abelard has abandoned the mythological terms and
explains the work of Christ in terms of human relationships. He has abandoned the objectionable idea that God

is somehow changed in his attitude by the work of Christ. But he has abandoned also the objective element in Christ's work. The work of Christ is completed only when we complete it, when we are moved by it and respond to it. All attempts to get rid of the mythological imagery run into the same difficulty. They leave us with an explanation in purely subjective terms.

There are many who do not regret this loss. For them it is sufficient that the work of Christ makes an effective change in the believer himself. They are prepared to let go the objective element in that work along with the mythological language that most of us find so difficult. They may be right in this, but it must be emphatically stated that the objective element in the work of Christ is one that the Church has always considered important. This is not in itself, perhaps, sufficient reason for preserving it at all costs, but it is sufficient reason for regarding its abandonment with apprehension.

We are obliged, I think, in this generation, to try to answer the question. 'How does the Atonement work?' We are obliged to try to present our understanding of the Atonement in non-mythological terms. But we must insist that in doing so we are describing merely the results of that work *in us*. We must insist that if this generation wishes to have that question answered *and in those terms*, we shall do our best, but that we are obliged to miss something out. If that something is to be included we can only include it by speaking unashamedly in the ancient language and by reciting the ancient myths, that Christ became a sacrifice on my behalf; that he has redeemed me from bondage to death and hell; that by his death he has purchased life for me; and that by his obedience my sin is atoned for. Only thus can we preserve the conviction of the Church that what has been done is done, whether we understand it or not, whether we believe it or not, whether we know it or not; that (in the words of Charles Wesley) 'For those *who would not come* to him, the ransom of his life was paid'.

IV

Let us then, having abandoned the traditional mythology, nevertheless try to answer the question as far as we are able: How does the work of Christ achieve its effect?

It is often asked, sceptically, 'How can an event of two thousand years ago affect me, now?' Put in that form (a form in which I have commonly heard it) it is an eminently and transparently silly question. It suggests that events of the past, or at least of the remote past, cannot affect the present—an idea that the most cursory study of history, or even a moment's common-sense reflection, is sufficient to dispose of. If the life and death of Jesus did no more, they have influenced the ideas, the moral values, the institutions, the culture of the whole Western world. It is manifestly impossible to say, *tout court*, that events of two thousand years ago cannot affect us now.

They have affected us and do affect us. (They have affected all who read this book, at least sufficiently to cause them to read about these events.)

But what lies behind the question is a much profounder and more serious difficulty. The real difficulty about the Atonement is not that the events that lie at the heart of it happened in the past. It is not the capacity of the past to influence the present that is the real issue. The question behind the question is, how can the life and the death on a cross of one man affect the relationship of another man to God?

To put it another way: Granted that guilt is something real—that I am guilty, or that I feel guilty, or that I recognize that I do not succeed in living up to my own ideals—how does the life and death of another man help me to get rid of my guilt, or to come to terms with it?

We must take our clue first of all from Abelard and say that if I see the life and death of Christ as the Church has taught me to see it, as an act of God, as a revelation by God, then it can clearly affect *my attitude* to my guilt and failure.

It can prompt me, first to regard the matter of my, guilt seriously, to treat it as significant. It can convince me that there is a way of looking at life, the New Testament's way, the Church's way, in which my guilt is one of the most significant things about me.

It can, secondly, convince me that the matter of my

guilt constitutes a problem that is not mine alone, but is shared with mankind at large.

Thirdly, it can bring me to see the matter of my guilt as a problem at once soluble and insoluble. Insoluble in that I shall always be a failure, that it is part of my humanity that I am fallible. Soluble in that the debilitating effects of guilt need no longer be felt.

The work of Christ, therefore, understood as the Church understands it, can affect me directly in that it changes my understanding of myself and of humanity at large. It can lead me to come to terms with myself.

One of the most striking things about humanity is its refusal to face the fact of its own failure. This can, of course, be heroic. But heroism can be wrong headed, even when it excites our imagination. Humanity's reluctance to face up to its failures is natural, since to face them negatively is debilitating and even degrading. But in Christ we learn how to face the facts of guilt and failure positively, to accept them, and to refuse to allow them to intimidate us.

In the novel *Henderson the Rain King* by Saul Bellow, we are given a picture of this human predicament. The novel is the history of a quest, the quest of its central character, Henderson, to free himself from the legacy of his own past failures.

The Christian is a man who has achieved this quest. He is not a man who is free from present sin or fallibility, or protected from those of the future. But he is man whose past is continually 'written off'. One might almost say that the first step in his rehabilitation is to learn to forgive himself.

So far we have followed the lead of Abelard. But there is something more to be said. The principal way in which the work of Christ has its effect on me, the direct historical connection between Jesus Christ and myself, is through his Church, and through its Scriptures and its sacraments. Jesus, by his life and death and resurrection, and by the coming of his Holy Spirit, created the Church. And the Church is both the instrument through which the significance of the work of Christ is proclaimed and also the community within which the results of that work can be apprehended.

For in the last resort the work of Christ is not something that can be understood as if it were a set of abstract propositions, as, let us say, a mathematical theorem can be understood, apart from one's personal involvement in it. The work of Christ can only be grasped by a man's entering the community in which the reorientation of his understanding becomes possible.

The Church is the community of those who are prepared to face the reality of sin and guilt and failure, in themselves and in the world, and to face the situation that these things have created. It is not the community of those who have got rid of sin and guilt for themselves (or who have managed to persuade themselves that they have got rid of them), but of those who have been freed from its debilitating effects, who are free to acknowledge: 'Yes, we are guilty.' 'Yes, we have done things of which we are ashamed.' 'Yes, we are that kind of people.' 'Yes, we shall no doubt sin and make mistakes again today.' We are humbled by this knowledge, but not depressed. We are convinced that there are possibilities for us even in our failure. The Church is the community of those who are prepared, in Luther's richly suggestive, richly misunderstood phrase, to 'be sinners, and to sin boldly'. We are those who are freed not only from illusion about ourselves, but from disillusion too. We see our guilt in proper perspective, as something serious, but not disastrous, interfering but not disabling, that can somehow be absorbed, at a cost, at a great cost—in a word, that can be forgiven.

This then is the real, the tangible, the concrete connection between that event two thousand years ago and me—the Church, the community in which this understanding becomes possible.

And what makes this understanding possible is not merely a set of explanations that the Church offers me. It is not a merely intellectual apprehension at all. The necessity of salvation and the possibility of salvation are grasped by becoming and remaining a member of the Church, and (which is another way of saying the same thing) by sharing in the sacraments of the Church.

The Christian answer to the problem of guilt is, then, that it is dealt with by the work of Christ, which is an

act of God himself. That act achieved something objective, which we could not achieve for ourselves. And the
work of Christ acts on us through the medium of the
community that he created. It is mediated to us not
only in intellectual understanding, in the preaching of
the Gospel, but in the water of his baptism and in the
sharing of his body and his blood.

5: The Sacraments

S. G. HALL

INTRODUCTION

THE word 'sacrament' does not present a problem of definition. Since it is scarcely used except to denote the Christian rites or to draw metaphors from them, to define it is a useless exercise. Passions are sometimes roused by the controversy about whether there are seven sacraments or two. But this is really a dispute about authority, between those who accept Roman Church tradition as authoritative, and those for whom the Bible is the sole norm. For the purposes of this essay it can be set aside. We shall not discuss the interesting but unenlightening history of the word, but rather use it to label certain ceremonies: baptism, or washing the body in the name of the Trinity; and communion, or sharing bread and wine in commemoration of Christ's death.

These sacraments seem to raise three sets of difficulties. The first concerns the general question: Why have sacraments at all? What part have such outward acts in pure religion? Why not do without them? Secondly, there are the interrelated problems of origin and divine authority. Can we still believe that Christ himself instituted the sacraments? If not, can we still believe that they are God's appointed means of union with him? Why *these* ceremonies and not others? The third set of objections and difficulties concerns the meaning of the rites. Theologians fight fiercely about what they mean—what are we to believe? If the true meaning is so obscure, should we not discard them? In discussing these last points there is room for something more positive than simply refuting objections.

Before we tackle the three sets of questions, one important thing should be said. The sacraments make no sense in isolation. They are part of a whole theological and historical complex. The complex cannot be understood apart from the sacraments, nor the sacraments apart from the rest. In particular, the sacraments have to be understood in relation to God, who created the world and men, to Christ his Son, who took flesh and died for our sins, and to the Catholic Church as an historical organization in which God confronts us more immediately as the Holy Spirit. Some difficulties about the sacraments are really difficulties about the concept of a living, personal God related to man in historical events, and are not primarily our concern. On the other hand, the wider aspects of the Gospel will be illuminated, and perhaps accepted or rejected, partly in the light of what the sacraments are and mean. For the most part, we shall take for granted the basic truths of historic Christianity, and interpret the sacraments in their light.

THE NEED FOR SACRAMENTS

The sacraments are symbolic acts. We do them, and they mean more than we do. Each is, to use an early Christian term, a *mysterion*; it has a meaning not obvious except to the initiated. That meaning is indicated or suggested by the words with which each ceremony is attended, though the words do not *state* the meaning, which is contained not in the words but in the act. The sacraments are symbolic acts, and that puts them in a class with many other human activities. For we are surrounded by societies that use ceremonial of various kinds, and our friendships and families are bonded by all sorts of symbolic acts. It is to this universal fact that we can appeal in the face of our first set of difficulties.

Our objector might say something like this:

Why are such outward acts necessary to true religion? It is clear from the start that the outward act is not identical with the inward meaning. It is possible on the one hand to perform the outward act with no sense of the inward meaning, with no spiritual perception of it, with no intention that the rite should be significant of a desire to obey and love God. On the other hand, it is equally possible to achieve the inward and spiritual graces of the sacraments without the outward rites. Whatever baptism signifies—repentance and forgiveness, adoption as God's child, and the like—must surely be available to many to whom baptism is not available. And the graces of communion—spiritual union with Christ in his perfect sacrifice with all that that entails—are available to many who do not communicate physically. We find this fact widely affirmed by theologians generally classed as evangelical. We find it demonstrated by the lives of saintly Quakers. We find it acknowledged in one form or another by traditional Catholic theology; martyrdom was always reckoned equivalent to baptism, and 'spiritual communion' at mass an approved devotional practice. So why not go whole-heartedly for what really matters, for the inward and spiritual? The outward acts merely confuse the issue. They distract us from the spiritual reality, and expose us to the danger of thinking that God delights in external religion rather than penitence and mercy and love in the heart. All else apart, the whole message of Jesus was just this, that the inward character, disposition, and intention are all-important, and that the outward things of religion are valueless.

In answer to our questioner we make two replies. The sacraments are needed because men are what they are, and they are needed because God is what he is.

We may approve or disapprove, but we can hardly deny the fact that human beings need significant ceremonies,

symbolic acts. Atheist Russia as well as hyper-religious
America puts garlands of flowers on its spacemen. Even
phlegmatic Englishmen like to see their Queen ride in a
golden coach and be crowned with mysterious symbolic
pomp. They march to cenotaphs with poppy-wreaths.
They burn Ministers of Agriculture in effigy. They carry
on the curious rites of the Freemasons and Buffaloes. In
more private matters, one must ask our objector whether
he would deny the value of an engagement ring on the
ground that without it the relation between the parties is
more clearly shown as pure love? In fact, our spiritual
relations with others invariably involve the physical act
at some point. A good friend can be a prisoner of war for
years, completely shut off from correspondence, and the
friendship, being a spiritual thing, be unimpaired. But a
friend who in more normal conditions of absence takes as
his attitude, 'We are friends, so you know that the merely
outward fact that I never answer your letters does not
alter the pure spiritual affection of my heart'—what do
we make of him? Human relations, inward and spiritual
as they are at their best, yet need outward and visible
expression. And it is the same in our relation to God.
We remain human, and our relation to God requires outward acts to express it; not merely acts of moral obedience
(though they are an essential element in true worship)
but symbolic acts as tokens of free love. This is all the
more true because our prime way of knowing God is
through contact with or membership of the Church,

where we know him as the Holy Spirit. Our bond with
God is also a bond with his people. Like any other human
association, the Church needs symbolic rituals that set
forth its nature and purposes, and these we call the
sacraments.

It could be replied at this point that our relation with
God is quite exceptional, and just because it is with God
it ought to be more pure and spiritual than our other
more carnal relations. In approaching God, we should
rise above bodily things.

This objection brings us conveniently to our second
point, which is that we need the sacraments because
God is what he is. It has already been pointed out that we
should have to call upon the broad background of
Christian theology, and we do so now. The Gospel makes
God known to us as the creator of an undeniably material
world which he loves and approves, and as the creator of
men and women who are physical beings and not dis-
embodied ghosts. We learn of God making himself
known in and through the material order, and principally
through what men do and experience in the events of
history. We learn that God's final and complete word to
man is not a system or a metaphysics or a code of rules,
but his own Son among us as Man: 'The Word became
flesh, and dwelt among us.' Thus in Jesus of Nazareth
God took to himself the whole of man's nature, purged
mankind of sin by his death, and transformed it into what
it was always intended to be, the perfect copy of his

own perfection. The body of the Son of God was as tangible and as vulnerable as yours and mine, of flesh and blood and bones. God stands not far off, as the distant destiny of refined souls, but near at hand, wrestling with the very flesh that is our pride and our terror. Now it is at least apt and fitting that such a God should prescribe outward rites as signs or instruments of his presence among us, now that the mortal body of Jesus is not here. And it makes sense that such a God, whose final word to man was a living man, should provide means of knowing him that are acts done and seen rather than words learnt and recited. And it is reasonable that such a God should expect us to meet him on his chosen ground, responding to symbolic acts of love with symbolic acts of love. And finally, if this is what God has required of us, it is not being spiritual to refuse him his due. Jesus says to us, 'God is a spirit, and they that worship him must worship him in spirit and in truth.' But he says also, 'I am the way, and the truth, and the life; no man cometh unto the Father but by me.' We may disapprove of God's methods, or disbelieve the Gospel; we can hardly have the Gospel and sweep aside the sacraments.

ORIGIN AND AUTHORITY

An uncommitted inquirer might well raise the question of authority or authentication. If (as we have said) the meaning of sacraments lies in the doing of them and not in the explanation of them, how does one know that they are true to God and his relation to man? Why baptize and not circumcize? Why bread and wine and not tea and biscuits? To this kind of question only one fundamental reply is possible: Because God so appointed it. If we think for a moment about God's relation to us we can see why this is so. God differs from us as creator from creature; we can be like him only as far as he accords that likeness to us. His ways are far above out of our sight; his thoughts are not our thoughts. He is the standard by which truth and art and conduct are judged. How then could man be wise enough and holy enough to give out the forms and ceremonies that are to enshrine the truth of God, to make his sanctifying presence accessible, to express God to man and man to God? Only God himself can appoint these things. This leads at once to a second difficulty, however: How do we know that God appointed the sacraments? Our knowledge of their origin is imperfect—more imperfect than most laymen imagine possible. Explanations of their origin can be given that exclude God's appointment as a factor altogether. We certainly cannot demonstrate that God appointed them and we should not attempt to do so. But we can and should be able to show that it is reasonable to believe that he did appoint them as a part of his grace towards men in Christ.

Earlier ages of Christendom found the question easier. God appointed the sacraments by a distinct, straightforward command. Just as in the Old Testament we read that God appeared to Moses on Mount Sinai and dictated the Law, moral and ceremonial, for Israel, so in the New Testament God himself, incarnate in Christ Jesus, commanded the rites that the Church must follow, dictating the basic formulae of words and action for their performance. The command to baptize in the threefold name you can read at Matthew xxviii. 19; the institution of the eucharist can be read at Matthew xxvi. 26–29 and 1 Corinthians xi. 24–25, with parallels in Mark and Luke. Whether they looked to the Church or to the Scriptures as their final religious authority, Christians used to get the same answer: *Dominus dixit*, Jesus said so, and it is therefore right. Historical criticism has not left that answer unchallenged. First, competent scholars have questioned whether the earliest accounts of the command to baptize (Matt. xxviii. 19) and the institution of the eucharist (1 Cor. xi. 24–25) were originally part of the document we found them in. Perhaps a later scribe read back his own Church practices into the Scripture he was copying. It is widely held that this did happen in Luke xxii. 17–20. If the text adopted in the Revised Standard Version and New English Bible is the right one, an original short version of the communion, with the wine distributed before the bread, has been filled up and reshaped in most ancient manuscripts, but not all. True, most scholars, including very sceptical ones, now believe we have Paul's and Matthew's texts intact; some even favour the longer reading of Luke. But that does not help much: the mere possibility of such corruption must be faced.

Secondly, allowing the integrity of the texts, a deeper problem emerges. How much of what the Bible attributes to Jesus did he actually say? Very few critically-minded scholars believe he actually said the baptismal words of Matthew xxviii. 19; they were attributed to the Master on the same grounds that all ceremonial law in the Old Testament, even that of late origin, was attributed to Moses. The same goes for the Pauline account of the last supper: it is widely held that Paul himself altered and enhanced the tradition, so that what had been a kind of holy social meal called bread-breaking became a sacrifice in which the participants feed upon the flesh and blood of God. Scholars cast their net wide in seeking the origins and contributing influences. For the Communion, the influence is alleged of Greek mystery religions, Jewish religious brotherhood meals, the Passover, and the table fellowship of Jesus with publicans and sinners. Baptism obviously owed something to John the Baptist, who baptized for remission of sins but not in the name of the Trinity; it may have owed something to Jewish purificatory washings, especially of converts, and to Greek mystery-cults, in which initiates died and rose again, or were born again, or were incorporated in the god, in a manner analogous to Christian baptism. And these are not much more than a sample of opinions. All of them

tend to lessen the importance of any actual institution by
Jesus himself. Many scholars have worked hard to vindi-
cate the view that he did institute the sacraments in
more or less the form recorded in the New Testament.
In the case of the communion, it can be maintained that
it was from the start a unique addition to the regular
Jewish religious meal, and was filled with sacrificial
meaning even on the night when Jesus was arrested.
Certainly, in the case of baptism, one could argue from
Paul's habit of associating the Father, the Son, and the
Spirit in baptismal contexts that our earliest evidence for
Christian baptism shows trinitarian content, if not form;
and this could be confirmed from the earliest account of
Jesus's baptism, where the Father, Son, and Spirit appear
together for the only time in Mark's Gospel (Mark i.
9–11). But suppose the more sceptical view is right, and
the Church did falsely attribute to Jesus words he never
said. We cannot honestly say that it is impossible. But can
we then believe that God appointed the sacraments?
I believe we can.

If the broad message of the Gospel is true, God is
neither remote from us in unqualified transcendence, nor
confined to an earthly appearance in the first century. He
is known not only as Father and Son, but as Spirit; he
spoke by prophets before, and lives in the Church after,
the time of Jesus. What the Church does humbly, and in
the 'spirit' (to use the word in a non-theological sense) of
Jesus, may be claimed as done with God's authority. This

authority will not be infallibility; the authority of God in the Church, as in the Bible, is an authority that shines through the varied and sometimes perverse attempts of man to evade or understand it. *How* that authority is expressed and identified in the Church is discussed elsewhere. Now, perhaps the Church attributed to Jesus those ceremonies that brought alive for them the experience of meeting him, of receiving in him and from him the life of God. If so, we must dissent from their historical judgement; Jesus did not say and do what they claim for him. But we cannot, if we believe the Gospel, doubt that their historical judgement was well aimed. For if it had not been for Jesus, then the particular kind of divine grace, God's presence and his very self, that they found in the society that does the sacraments, would not have existed. The Church did owe the sacraments to the Son of God. Further, we may recall that the Church took more seriously than we do the truth of the Lord's resurrection; he was alive among his people, teaching them by the Spirit that spoke in prophets and teachers and pastors. The baptismal command of Matt. xxviii. 19 is given by the risen Christ. If we have any part in their faith that he lives for ever, we can still recognize in the sacraments of the Church God's authority and the grace of his own present action, world without end.

WHAT DO THE SACRAMENTS MEAN?

We shall not expect a small part of a single lecture to do what innumerable edifying sermons and controversial books have failed to do, namely, to produce a final and lucid exposition of what the sacraments mean. Rather, what we say is bound to indicate the immense variety of faith and opinion about them. If this widens our view of the subject, so much the better. But the variety can be bewildering, and may for some be a stumbling-block. If, we may ask, the difficulty of saying what good the sacraments do or represent is so great; if great scholars and saints even disagree about whether the sacraments do anything or merely represent something; then what is the humble believer to believe? How is he to know which is right? In an age of ecumenical churchmanship he cannot honestly fall back on the refrigerated textbook responses of one denomination or party. Are the Baptists right or the Congregationalists? The evangelicals or the Anglo-Catholics? The Calvinists or the Papists? At this point our humble believer, if his faith is not deeply rooted in another part of the Christian complex, may choose the way of the humble disbeliever. For if opinions and explanations contradict each other, does not that suggest that the whole procedure is meaningless, defying rational justification? We consider first one question that affects both sacraments, and then consider them separately.

There are those who claim that sacraments are merely signs, while others insist that they are also instruments. It is the difference between a flag and a sword, or between a garage-sign and a petrol-pump: one *shows* something, the other *does* something, or rather we use the sign to show something, and the instrument to do something. It is very difficult in fact to think of a sign that is not also an instrument, or an instrument that is not significant as well as useful. Nevertheless, the distinction broadly applies in the case of the sacraments. When we baptize a man, do we make him something he was not before—regenerate, a member of the Church, or the like—or do we merely show what he truly is already—a child of God, either because of God's eternal purpose, or because of his recent conversion? Is the eucharist a sacrifice made, or a visual aid to understand the sacrifice made once long ago? The probability is that we shall never be able to answer definitely that the sacraments are signs or are instruments. It may well be that they fit both categories well and neither wholly. This is as it should be, if they are truly to be the medium of God's loving relation to man. If we treat them as purely instrumental and forget that they point to something beyond themselves, we shall underestimate God. For if by doing something we are able to manipulate the relation between God and man, regardless of whether there is any spiritual insight, then we have God in our control; the sacrament is purely magic, and does not leave room for the essentially personal element in the relation. This personal element, the enlargement of the self through confronting another, is *desirable* in dealing with other people and *inescapable* in dealing with the living, transcendent God. It is to such misunderstanding of the sacraments that the word of Jesus applies: 'It is the spirit that gives life; the flesh is of no avail' (John vi. 63). On the other hand, we dare not deny to God the power and the will to present himself to us in concrete, material ways; the Word became flesh and God intends to make available to us in Christ not just signs of his presence, but himself. Perhaps it is here that the reason lies for the difficulty. God made the world contingent and temporary, and remains God transcendent. It is his nature to be found in the world, and yet to be above it. So in the sacraments God is present and active, yet is not caught within them, but transcends. Many of the difficulties fall away when we remember that it is not primarily we that act in the sacraments. Our part is real—I should say really an act and really a sign—but it is secondary. It is God who acts; whatever we do, we do in his name, on his authority. In the teeth of the difficulty we have considered, that of reconciling the sacraments as signs with the sacraments as instruments, there is no surer way to avoid error that to remember that it is God who uses them.

There remain further controversies to confound our humble believer. First, there is the wide difference of opinion about baptism. Is it a necessary rite to wash away from babies their original sin, and give them a hope of eternal life should they die young? Is it an outward and visible testimony by a comprehending adult of his personal faith in Christ? Or is some more complex and subtle view to be adopted? To anyone troubled by these controversies there are at least three things to say. The first is that differences of theological opinion arise from the vitality of the sacraments, which extends its truth in various fruitful directions. Baptism was never simply and universally understood in the Church. In the New Testament itself, it betokens among other things the washing-away of sin, the gift of the Holy Spirit, incorporation into Christ, dying and rising with Christ, putting on Christ like a robe, and being born again. In the primitive Church the evidence that babies were baptized is to some overwhelming, to others negligible; it seems quite likely that in this, as in other matters, variety came first and consistency later. The act is itself so rich in meaning that any explanation either fails to do it justice or contradicts some other aspect of it. The second thing to say is that baptism is not an affair for the individual only. Many difficulties are caused—for instance, the question whether the Holy Spirit is given in baptism or not—through leaving out the factor of solidarity. In the matter of original sin, which baptism can be thought to remove, it is not a question of thinking unkindly of a poor innocent baby. It is rather a question of belonging to a sinful human race, which the baby can no more help

than he can help being English or German or Pakistani or
whatever the case may be. And his rebirth or receiving
the Spirit is not an individual thing like his diphtheria
injection; it is rather incorporation into (or declaring in-
corporate in) the new humanity, the Spirit-filled people.
This is the point on which one may lay weight in talking
to anyone who is not baptized, and believes that he or she
need not be, on the ground that in other respects, by
conversion and Church membership, all is done that God
requires. None of us dare say, 'I am not as other men
are'. At least we may not, if we are to be disciples of
Jesus, who though sinless received the baptism of John
for the remission of sins, and on the Cross endured the
consequences of identifying himself with sinful humanity. In truth, it is by owning our solidarity with other
men, by saying, 'We have sinned with our fathers', that
we truly repent and begin to imitate Jesus. Thirdly, in
the divided state of the Church, each person should accept
humbly and loyally the discipline of one particular
denomination, but not pretend that it has the monopoly
of divine truth on the subject. He must express his
solidarity with all men in sin, and with the universal
Church in God's righteousness, by baptism within a
specific congregation of the people of God. But in the
light of the primitive and continuing variety of interpretation, he dare not presume to know the whole truth.
The Lord bade us test prophets and teachers by their
fruits: if the fruits mean sanctity, he would be a rash

man to claim a monopoly, or even a statistically significant preponderance, for any particular Christian
body.

In the case of the communion we may again be perplexed by the divergent views of saints and scholars.
some insist that in the ceremony the bread and wine
remain bread and wine; others that they become the body
and blood of Christ; others that they do both; others that
they become so for believers only, or that their benefits
accrue only to the faithful recipient. Some insist that the
act of breaking and sharing bread and passing round the
cup, not the bread and wine themselves, constitutes the
sacrament. Others insist that the principal act is not the
sharing but the consecrating in the hand of a qualified
priest, which is a sacrifice acceptable to God for the sins
of the living and the dead. Others allow a sacrifice, but as
the act of the whole Church as it participates in the one
sacrifice of Jesus. Others deny that it is proper to speak of
sacrifice at all. And so on. Those who, in the face of such
divergence, are disposed to pursue their discipleship, are
perhaps best advised to remember that the act says more
than any of the words. They may legitimately attempt to
frame for themselves a doctrine, but should remain at
heart reverent—almost agnostic—about such a mystery.
But what about the one who suspects that the divergence
is due to a basic incoherence, and finds the disputes
(quite apart from the acrimony with which they were
and are conducted) themselves constituting an objection

to belief? The answer is again threefold. First, as in the case of baptism, the divergence of opinion is due in part to the very richness of the rite. In the New Testament and the primitive Church, we can detect several elements contributing to the power of the mystery. It is a meal that Jesus ate with his friends, and is like many others he ate with all sorts of men in his ministry. It has special, universal significance indicated by the stories of miraculous feeding of great crowds in the desert. It is inexorably linked with the Jewish Passover, though whether the last supper was a Passover meal or not is a subject of disagreement even between the four Gospels. Some things suggest that the communion began as an ordinary meal with a grace; others that the specific words of institution always were unique and sacrificial. Overshadowing all are the Old Testament conception of a covenant between God and man, and the central point of the Gospel, the crucifixion of Jesus himself. And what begins in the New Testament has been continued and further explored as the years pass. G. Dix wrote in a striking passage:[1]

Men have found no better thing than this to do for kings at their crowning and for criminals going to the scaffold; for armies in triumph or for a bride and bridegroom in a little country church; for the proclamation of a dogma or for a good crop of wheat; for the wisdom of the Parliament of a mighty nation, or for a sick old woman afraid to die; for a schoolboy sitting an examination or

[1] *The Shape of the Liturgy*, p. 744.

for Columbus setting out to discover America; for the famine of whole provinces or for the soul of a dead lover; in thankfulness because my father did not die of pneumonia; for a village headman much tempted to return to fetich because the yams had failed; because the Turk was at the gates of Vienna; for the repentance of Margaret; for the settlement of a strike; for a son for a barren woman; for Captain so-and-so, wounded and prisoner of war; while lions roared in the nearby amphitheatre; on the beach at Dunkirk; while the hiss of scythes in the thick June grass came faintly through the windows of the church; tremulously, by an old monk on the fiftieth anniversary of his vows; furtively, by an exiled bishop who had hewn timber all day in a prison camp near Murmansk; gorgeously, for the canonisation of S. Joan of Arc . . .. And best of all, week by week, and month by month, on a hundred thousand successive Sundays, faithfully, unfailingly, across all the parishes of Christendom, the pastors have done this just to *make* the *plebs sancta Dei*—the holy common people of God.

The deed itself carries within it the life of Christ, who gave his flesh for the life of the world. We should not be surprised if our explanations prove futile or self-contradictory.

There remain two reasons for continuing to believe in the teeth of theological disputes. As with baptism, one is a question of solidarity. The communion expresses and in some sense brings about the unity of men in Christ. If they differ about what it is and how it works, it remains a sharing in the life of Christ, who died to draw all men into one in likeness to himself. If men remain men, and quarrel while they are still being sanctified, that does not affect the reality of what they quarrel over. You do not refuse an effective medicine because doctors differ about its precise mode of acting on the body. It is not the disputes of scholars, but real evidence that conducting this rite tends in the long run to make men more bitter and wicked to each other, that would constitute a real objection; and whatever the depravity of churchmen, that would be difficult to demonstrate. The other reason is that even in a divided Church we are offered by God real, if incomplete, fellowship in a society of believers. Whether or not we agree with its theology of the eucharist, we can give to one denomination our loyalty and disciplined obedience, and we can use and explore what we do not yet understand, praying as we do that the true unity which the communion expresses, the union of all men in Christ, may be fulfilled.

SOME POSITIVE CONSIDERATIONS

It would be wrong to leave the impression that those who discuss the sacraments invariably or usually do so in a contentious spirit. It may have been true in the past. Nowadays, however, a conciliatory spirit is abroad. Some long-standing disputes can now be seen in perspective as the results of prejudices and presuppositions that were shared by the contending parties. By penetrating behind the disputes and understanding them historically it is often possible to escape the rigidities of long-established positions. Moreover, the historical quest is itself an activity that heirs of the disputing parties can honourably and usefully share. In eucharistic theology, for example, the reformers and the Roman Catholics shared the view that, if the communion is an offering made to God, it is in some sense a repetition of or addition to the sacrifice of Christ. The Romans stuck to the idea of an offering, and accepted the consequence that the priest at mass really offers Christ as a sacrifice for the sins of men. The reformers denied the possibility of such a sacrificial priesthood as being a pagan and anti-Scriptural conception, and felt obliged to reject with it the notion of an offering. With wider historical knowledge and better critical techniques it is now possible to see that the early Church had an idea of eucharistic offering that avoided the Reformation dilemma. They saw it as an offering made by the Church as a whole, and by all its members, not by a professional priest on the Church's behalf. It was regarded not as an addition to Christ's perfect offering of himself for the sins of all the world, nor as a repetition of it, but as a partaking in it. What Christ does once for all, he does in and through all. This is the kind of theology we meet in what is called the Liturgical Movement. In that movement and in the theological quest that lies behind it, Protestants and Roman Catholics alike take part. This is one instance of many that could be cited, of common ground being discovered through the study of the sacraments historically.

We cannot survey the whole field of sacramental theology. Too much is happening in the rediscovery of the thought of the Biblical and early Christian tradition. And the theological consequences of Pope John's *aggiorn-amento* are only beginning to appear. But some things may help those with difficulties, and two are worth considering. They are the historical and the eschato-logical dimensions of the sacraments.

First, the historical dimension. When God gave his Son into the hands of men, he committed himself to events that can be historically related and examined. One of the consequences of this is that the evidence for the events of Jesus's life is subject to the uncertainties of historical transmission, of the kind described in the discussion of authority (see p. 132–141). His life had itself an historical background, and became part of the history of those who came after. Its background was primarily the history of the people of the old covenant—Israel, with its institu-tions, traditions, and Scriptures. On the night of his arrest, Jesus was one of many who had gathered at Jerusalem to celebrate Passover, the annual commemor-ation and renewal of the deliverance of Israel from Egypt. But the Passion and rising of Jesus became themselves the momentous history of the new people of God, the Church. The Church looks back to Jesus not only as the fulfilment of Israel's hopes for a coming King, but as one

who fulfilled all the will of God, the proper man who
presented before God and man what man in God's purpose truly is. The sacraments do for the Church what the
Passover and other festivals did for the Israelites. The
momentous events of the past are brought to life and
applied to an actual congregation or individual. St.
Paul teaches his friends that in their baptism they were
baptized into the death of Christ, so that just as Jesus
died to sin and rose to new life, so the believer may pass
through a moral death to a new life of righteousness
(Romans vi. 1–11). What Christ did once for all to satisfy
the righteousness of God, each and every Christian does
by his baptism and the life that flows from it. Similarly,
the holy communion is performed 'in remembrance of'
Jesus. Just as the Jews relived the deliverance from
Egypt at each Passover, so the members of the Church
relive the night when Jesus was betrayed, his crucifixion
and rising, each time they perform his appointed memor-
ial. They set forth for God and man to see the greatest of
the acts of God; they rejoice at the privilege of sharing,
individually and congregationally in the life of Christ.

But Christ and his disciples always looked ahead as well
as behind. They thought about the future, the ultimate,
significant future, as well as about the past and its
meaning. They had a doctrine about the last things—
what theologians call an eschatology. Their thoughts
about the sacraments were shaped by this, and so should
ours be.

Baptism represents to John the Baptist and to the Church of Christ a preparing for the last judgement. He who takes the cleansing offered, repenting from the heart, need not fear the searing flames of God's judgement, which burns up what is evil like chaff. To the Church, but not to John, it also represents the gift of the Holy Spirit, who comes upon God's people to raise them from the death of sin to the new heavenly life as God's children—a life they are to live progressively in this age, triumphantly in the next. Translated into the more metaphysical terms in which my paper is expressed, this means that our baptism assures us that we belong ultimately, utterly, to God. He has plans for the future. But they are not plans that imply that he is absent, or that he withholds himself from us now. Rather, his cleansing, his life, his very self, are ours if we walk in the Spirit. We live in this world, but our citizenship is in heaven, in the age to come; which means we can conquer this world, and enjoy it and exploit it as the children of this world, prisoners of worldly affections, cannot.

When the Lord instituted the communion, he swore that he would not partake of it again till God's kingdom comes. And as St. Paul says, 'as often as ye eat this bread and drink this cup, ye do show the Lord's death till he come (1 Cor. xi. 26). To the first Christians, the breaking of the bread was a presence, a coming of Christ that foreshadowed, gave a foretaste of, the final coming when all things are fulfilled according to God's original high purpose for his creation. The little things upon the table, the little people round it, are taken up into the living Christ; the bread and wine shared in his name are our precious sign that in the end all things are his, and through them glory is given to the Father. I have yet to see any evidence that this hope is out of date.

CONCLUSION

The sacraments, we may conclude, are needed because men are men who need concrete acts and signs to express themselves to each other and to God, and because God himself appoints such acts as his meeting-ground with us. The consequences of criticism are not such that we are compelled to reject the idea of divinely appointed ceremonies. Disputes over the meaning of the sacraments do not bring their usefulness into question or make their humble use impossible. And we may accept them gratefully as God's pledges to us of the reality of what he has done for every man in the historic past, and what he intends for all men in the eternal future.

6: *The Church*

J. S. BOWDEN

ONE brand of popular literature has made the interior of the study of the President of the United States as familiar as more public American landmarks. Inside the oval room, with its thick carpets and pale-green walls, stands the President's desk, and on it, amidst the memoranda and electronic paraphernalia of modern communication, there is said to be a card with a simple reminder: 'The buck stops here.'

The motto deserves an equally prominent place in any account of the difficulties that the Church presents, whether to the Christian believer or to the unbeliever. For a whole set of difficulties, which have appeared in various forms throughout this series, looks for a final resolution outside the realm of Christian doctrine, in the world of Christian experience, in the Church. In the Church, talk becomes action, vision becomes reality, each illuminated by the other—or it does not. The new life, reconciliation, forgiveness, grace, sanctification, are shown to be present possibilities—or they are not. The whole point of Christian doctrine is that it is not about what ought to happen or what believers would like to be true, but about what has happened and does happen, and is true. If the Christian cannot say at some point, in support of his argument, 'But look here!', his case must be seriously weakened, and he will never dispel a nagging suspicion that it is all just talk after all.

So one task in any account of the Church is to give a reminder that what Christians claim goes for very little unless it is reflected in what they do and are seen to do. Consequently, one important area of difficulties will be practical ones, which arise from the character of the Church as it is today, and no amount of lectures will be of the slightest use in resolving them unless they are tackled on a practical level.

Before we get this far, however, two other problems have to be considered. It is no longer self-evident in the context of modern society that to be a Christian one has to belong to the Church. The Church, as an organized body, is open to a great deal of suspicion, criticism, and resentment. Its continued existence may be thought to be a tribute to its own powers of self-preservation rather than to the special qualities of the life led within it. So some answer must be given to the question 'Why have a Church at all?'

Secondly, the word 'Church' cannot be left as vague as it has been so far. Used without further definition, it is

open to considerable misinterpretation, and it begs a
number of important questions. So we must also ask
what 'the Church' is.

So the difficulties group themselves round three central questions, which can best be taken in reverse order to
that in which they have been raised: What is 'the
Church'? Is it still necessary in twentieth-century
secular society? And if so what form should it take?

'Church' is one of those slippery words that are so
difficult to pin down in theological writings. Like other
apparently simple words that Christians use, it can occur
in so many ways, in so many different contexts, that it
often becomes virtually impossible to identify the reality
to which it refers. The complexity of the word 'Church'
in particular is the greater because it is used at a number
of different levels, and it is all too easy for these levels to
be confused.

We talk readily enough of 'the Church' as the body of
Christ, as *the* place where Christ's work of atonement is
made real in us, as *one* society. We can hardly avoid doing
so. But in its empirical form the Church is manifestly
not one. If we look for some visible society that corres-
ponds to the terms in which we habitually feel drawn to
describe 'the Church', we find no unity, but a plurality of
denominations that are regularly, though misleadingly,
referred to as 'the Churches', and are notable as much
for this lack of unity as for anything else. If as a result we
alter the question slightly and go on to ask, 'But *which* is

the Church?', there are those who will be eager to give us a definite answer, with arguments to back it up, but more thoughtful replies will display a reluctance to answer the question as it has been put.

There is, in fact, no simple straightforward answer to be had. The Church, whatever else it is, is composed of people, generations of people, and that means that it has a history, Small communities in every country, and especially in America, have tried to frame a definition of the Church and to use it as a fresh starting-point, but the background of two thousand years of history makes a mockery of their exclusive claims. All the contexts in which we talk about 'the Church' have their roots in that history, and if we want to learn what 'the Church' is, it is to that history that we must turn.

The beginning of the Christian Church is Jesus Christ. So much is plain. What perhaps is not so plain is the way in which he is this beginning. The Church is not an organization founded by a group of men who gathered together to perpetuate the memory and follow the ideals of Jesus of Nazareth. Nor is it a ghastly mistake, an institutionalization of the spiritual message of an inspired prophet. It is even doubtful, though this is more vigorously disputed, whether we are justified in regarding the Church as an organization, a society founded and prepared for by the historical Jesus during his life on earth. Despite the arguments of many distinguished scholars, the evidence would seem insufficient to compel this conclusion, and even if it were stronger, it could be argued that to limit one's approach to the New Testament record to the question 'Did Jesus found the Church?' is not necessarily the best method.

St. Paul's epistles, the earliest documents that we have from the Church put the matter in a different way: the Church is not founded by Jesus, but on Christ. Indeed, they go even further and suggest that there is a way in which the Church *is* Christ.

Such compressed theological statements need to be clarified, and this is best done by drawing attention to the setting in which they were made. When we go back to these earliest parts of the New Testament, we find the life and worship of various congregations, conscious (or being reminded) that they are part of a larger community. This community is bubbling over with new life, responding to an experience without precedent, which it believes from the start to have implications for the whole world. It is by no means sure what these implications are; it is not even sure of its status *vis-à-vis* the other, larger, community, Judaism, to which its earliest members also belonged, and there is dispute about the terms on which new members are to be admitted. Many of the questions that demanded its attention, whether doctrinal or practical, could not be answered on any obvious authority, even that of Jesus himself, and have to be hammered out by what in some cases might almost be called a process of trial and error.

The creativity of the Church in this situation was quite remarkable. In its work of critical reflection upon its experience it used a wealth of contemporary and traditional images and ideas, including many of those that have become so much a part of our Christian vocabulary today. To regulate its life, it developed a wide variety of ministries and different systems of Church order. No one who has not studied the New Testament in depth can be fully aware of the complexities of the events that underline the apparently ordered and serene picture of primitive Christianity in the Acts of the Apostles. It just was not the case, as that picture suggests, that from the word 'Go' the way forward for the Church was clear, simple, and divinely dictated. Equally, no one who has not studied the Gospels can realize just how ready the early Church seems to have been to put words into the mouth of Jesus, to be free in drawing its pictures of him.

The source of this new life, this inspired freedom, is clear. It has grown up as a response to the resurrection of Jesus Christ from the dead. Jesus is more than a figure from the past; he is one who is still present as a living Lord. And it is the transition from a group of people who knew and heard and followed Jesus of Nazareth to a community that after his death and burial knew him to be alive and in their midst that marks the birth of the Church. There is a complex here that resists attempts to unravel it. We saw earlier in this series how difficult it is to take the resurrection in isolation and demonstrate it, defend it, vindicate it, by itself, as a historical event. The nature of the events that are involved in the complex, and the very quality of the response of the earliest Church to Jesus, both stand in the way of our reconstructing the transition step by step.

Nevertheless, despite the freedom that leads to this historical uncertainty, there were also limits to the Church's response. Its new life was not just *a* new life, any more than it responded to the resurrection as *a* resurrection. It was new life in *Jesus Christ*, who had once walked the earth as a human individual; it was the resurrection of *Jesus*, whose character had been known and whose teaching had been heard and seen beforehand by those who acknowledged him as Lord. He stood over against the Church, an earthly figure who preceded it and was independent of it, as well as a risen Lord over it and within it, causing it to interpret his significance afresh. And it is a testimony to the fidelity of the early Church to its memory of Jesus that despite the many ways in which his person was interpreted, modern historical scholarship can still discern through these interpretations at least some distinct characteristics of the earthly Jesus, however much dispute there must be over details, and stubbornly refuses to abandon the quest to find him.

Nor, in this picture of widespread freedom, must we ignore the fixed points provided by the sacraments of baptism and the eucharist. It is extraordinarily difficult to trace them back to their origin, as we have seen, but there can be no question of their importance and their constant place in the life of the earliest Church.

It would be tempting from these illustrations to see the early days of the Church as halcyon days, a time that has not been equalled since, and the temptation has been a constant one. It might appear that the Church of that time is one, and the Church is holy. How can those who are in Christ be anything else? St. Paul's famous picture of the body of Christ is developed in glowing terms in the Epistle to the Ephesians, 'There is one body and one Spirit, just as you were called to the one hope that belongs to your call, one Lord, one faith, one baptism, one God and Father of us all, who is above all and through all and in all' (Eph. iv, 4–8). Again, St. Paul's description of the Corinthians as 'enriched in every way in Christ Jesus with all speech and knowledge', so that they are 'not lacking in any spiritual gift, as those who will be guilt-less in the day of our Lord Jesus Christ' (1 Cor. i, 5–8), is taken up in the words of 1 Peter: 'a chosen race, a royal priesthood, a holy nation, God's own people' (1 Peter, ii, 9).

But we must be careful to remember that this is only one side of the picture. There were divisions in Corinth, as there were divisions elsewhere. Indeed, it is quite likely that we are to see in the events underlying the disputes between Hellenists and Hebrews and the appointment of the Seven, described in Acts vi, the first schism in the Church. Nor are the saints of Corinth, and elsewhere, free from even the cruder moral shortcomings.

Here is the first hint of a paradoxical tension in the existence of the Church, as in the life of the individual, which is rooted (once again, as we have seen earlier in these lectures) in the character of the Atonement, in the tension between the objective nature of Christ's work and the need for it to be appropriated in the community of the Church. The indicative of what the Church *is* in Christ must be accompanied by an imperative, for the Church has yet to become what it is. The language that identifies the Church with the body of Christ cannot be divorced from the language that makes it all too plain what the visible Church has still to achieve.

It has been necessary to dwell on these aspects of the early Church at some length in order to establish three points that have an important bearing on what follows They are, in short:

First, that the Church did not appear fully organized and aware of its task; it was not born like Athene, who sprang fully-armed from the head of Zeus, but had to learn about its own nature as its members reflected on their experience and what led up to it.

Secondly, the norms by which the earliest Church organized its life were by no means simple ones. A number of different factors have to be taken into account.

Thirdly, even at this stage there was a tension between the language that the Church felt compelled by its experience to use about itself and the everyday life of its members.

All this we learn from the New Testament, and to this extent the New Testament also has normative value for us. But it follows that even the New Testament is therefore not a simple, straightforward norm to use, any more that the Church that it describes. If this was the period in which the Church *began* its work of reflecting upon its own experience, it is also the case that while there will be elements in that experience that are shown most plainly in the New Testament, there will also be points at which we must move beyond the New Testament Church's self-understanding.

The New Testament is itself part of a process of consolidation, when as a consequence of its own theology and of outside pressures (the two factors cannot always be separated easily) the Church was settling down to a continued existence in the world and was developing a regular ministry and a more coherent structure. This was an inevitable and indeed necessary step forward, a development without which no new movement that expresses itself in a visible community can survive, and it is a particularly welcome sign that the legitimacy of the development no longer needs to be defended as vigorously as in an earlier period of modern New Testament theology.

But again, in outlining this consolidation it is important to keep a true perspective. If the next few centuries saw a fuller realization of external unity in the Church than the periods either before or afterwards, this unity was far from being complete. Nor did the movement towards it proceed everywhere at the same rate or to the same extent. Here too there were schisms and divisions, and the tension between what the Church could be seen to be and what it was believed to be was exaggerated, ignored, prematurely resolved. This period sees the beginning of further difficulties about the Church which still continue to trouble us.

As reflection upon the Church continues, and the New Testament beginnings are elaborated, the *idea* of the Church takes on a more elaborate form and leads a life to some extent distinct from its original connection with the empirical Church. The character of the original tension is changed, and in many writers, particularly those influenced by Platonic or Gnostic thought (though this is not limited to them alone), the problem is put in terms of how the Church as a theological, spiritual reality is related to the visible Church.

Efforts to relate the two sides, once the problem has taken this form, can be seen most clearly in the sphere of discipline. If the Church is the bride of Christ, without spot or wrinkle, it is argued, then the Church must be composed of pure, spiritual men; there is no room inside it for the sinner. Similarly, if the Church is one, then those who for any reason dissent from the Church's authority are outside the Church, with all the consequences that that entails. And the necessary practical measures are implemented.

Alternatively, the true Church is seen as consisting of members of the empirical Church, but not all of them. True membership is limited to those who are perfect. Others may seem to be within the Church, but they do not really belong to it. Both these approaches can be found time and again in the period between the second and fifth centuries.

But at this time, despite the various attempts to solve the problem, which frequently led to schism, a firm hold was kept on the recognition that the Church is above all a visible reality. The importance of its existence as a visible reality may have been under-emphasized, but it was never lost. The Church, as a corporate body, stood over against the world, and the Christian did not live apart from the Church, Catholic or schismatic.

When the same issues came up again at the Reformation and in the period afterwards, however, the matter was very different. The reformers felt that the existing Church had become too corrupt to be called the body of Christ. For guidance they turned back to the New Testament and the discussions of the early Church. But their desire to break away from the stress on historical continuity, which dominated the thought of the Catholic Church, led them to distinguish between the visible and what we must now call the invisible Church in a new way. The 'true' Church is to be found wherever it embodies and expresses the invisible Church. As Calvin puts it in the *Institutes*: 'Wherever we see the word of

God sincerely preached and heard, wherever we see the sacraments administered according to the institution of Christ, there we cannot have any doubt that the Church of God has some existence' (IV. i. 9). Exactly the same form of words is also to be found in Luther.

Because these remarks are now made outside the historical continuity of the Church and seem to do away with the need for historical continuity, they open the way to a number of false developments. Once the theological *idea* of the Church replaces the visible Church as the foundation of the discussion, and this discussion is taking place in a fully Christianized society, the very existence of an organized Church is eventually a matter to be justified. There is no reason why the Church should be *visibly* one, why it should not split into thousands of separate sects.

It is only a short step from here to the view of the Church as 'event', put forward by Karl Barth and Rudolf Bultmann, and continued by their successors. Here the Church is made up of those who respond in faith to Christ as proclaimed in the Word. But as this faith-relationship is constituted and dissolved, apparently the same group of people can sometimes be the Church and sometimes not. As Dr. Hodgson has remarked, the existence of the Church on earth is thus like that of the Cheshire Cat.

There are important insights into Christianity in these developments, but at the end of them it is hardly surprising that the assertion 'I can be a Christian without going to Church' can be so common and so difficult to refute at all briefly. Its roots are deep ones.

Before we tie up the threads of this part and look again directly at the question 'What is the Church?' in the light of this survey, there is a footnote to be added about another factor in the Church's theology which is equally responsible for present difficulties. That is the basic pre-supposition that the Church exists for the salvation of its own members.

The Church's work was regarded from the start as the bringing of salvation. The first community described its experience as that of being freed from the domination of the powers of this world, as being 'saved' from judge-ment, from the wrath to come. These were the benefits of belonging to the Christian community, and to obtain them the natural step was to join that community. No one would have thought otherwise. And this presupposi-tion, that salvation is for the members of the community, has been the spur to the Church's missionary work throughout its long history.

But transfer this idea to the present situation, to a post-Christian Western society, where so many of the insights of Christianity have been secularized, and how does it look? Are we still to believe that a handful of people who are ready to accept ecclesiastical authority, certain patterns of religious behaviour, certain ideas and doctrines, perhaps because they are more credulous, more

fond of ecclesiastical activities, less fulfilled in other
directions, are 'saved', whereas others are not? Twentieth-century tolerance, the different terms in which we
habitually think, prevents most of us from putting the
issue as bluntly as that. But there is much left in Christian
theological thinking that has such a belief as a tacit pre-
supposition, and those outside the Church tenaciously
cling to the idea that this is what the Church is all
about.

Now if the Church's task, the task of theology, is to
reflect critically upon its experience—if, as I have argued,
it did not begin with a fully developed constitution, but
has changed in response to situations and advances in our
knowledge of society and of the world, as well as in
response to its growing knowledge of itself and its Lord—
then here, surely, is one area where revision is needed. Of
course there is a sense in which the Church *is* salvation,
in that it is, and exists, as the fruit of God's work in
Christ through the Holy Spirit, and it needs no further
justification for its existence other than that it is the
community in which that work is carried on. But our
prime need at present is to stress an equally important
truth that the body of Christ, like Jesus Christ himself,
breaks down all other patterns of human thought and
human community, and exists, not for the sake of its
members, but for the sake of those who do not yet have
its vision and experience of how things really are.

So the Church's members must be continually conscious of Christ's work of salvation, but not claim it exclusively for themselves; they are to live out their realization of its consequences in their own lives, drawing attention to it in what they do and what they are, but not forcing the world to join them on their own terms or be damned. Karl Barth has a fine passage to this effect in another context, in his commentary on the Epistle to the Romans: 'In Jesus we have discovered and recognized the truth that God is found everywhere and that, both before and after Jesus, men have been discovered by Him. In Him we have found the standard by which all discovery of God and all being discovered by Him is made known as such; in Him we recognize that this finding and being found is the truth of the order of eternity. Many live their lives in the light of redemption and forgiveness and resurrection; but that we have eyes to see their manner of life we owe to the One.'[1]

Now if it follows from this that working outwards, for others, is the aspect of the Church that needs to be stressed, then that fact, in itself, would seem to demand the existence of a Church, the Church, as a visible, organized body. And if one adds to this what we have seen from the earlier discussion, that theology is not a matter of applying simple norms, like an inherent infallible authority vested in the Church from the beginning, Word of God, teaching of the Fathers, present experience,

[1] K. Barth (trans. E. C. Hoskyns), *The Epistle to the Romans*, p. 97.

but reflection upon the life of the Christian community in the particular society in which it exists, not only in the light of its own history, but against the secular knowledge available to that age, it also seems essential for the vindication of Christian claims that there should be a continuing context of Christian community life, work, and worship recognizably related to the complex from which Christianity grew, however different it may be in details. In short, even in modern secular society, with its diffused acceptance of Christian insights, Christianity stands or falls by the existence of a visible Church. And that means a Church that is organized, and has links all over the world as well as with its historical past. Of course this Church will have a ministry—if I have not discussed, and do not intend to discuss, questions of ministry here it is because I believe them to be subsidiary to the doctrine of the Church, and not vice versa.

Important as this conclusion is, however, it still does not give a direct answer to the question 'What is "the Church"'? If it is essentially a visible body of people, where is it to be found?

The evidence seems to point in only one possible direction. We have seen a tension between the empirical Church and the theological idea of the Church right from the beginning, and the present situation may be different in degree, as a result of the course of history, but it is not necessarily different in kind, from the situation of the early Church. It is impossible to identify any one of the existing fragments into which the Church has broken, even of those who have maintained the most obvious links with the historical past in order and worship, as 'the Church'. For when we talk about 'the Church' in this way we are talking about something that is and yet is not. Like the individual, the Church is *simul justus et peccator*, a paradox that cannot be resolved (and it is amazing, as a number of scholars have pointed out, how the Reformers, who saw this truth so clearly in the personal realm, did not extend it to the doctrine of the Church). It is clear that those Churches that do not have a firm historical succession and traditional Church order equally preserve important aspects of the truth and are in no way inferior or second-class communities.

History, whatever its importance, can prove a burden as well as a source of strength, and we suffer, not only from past misinterpretations of it, which have identified the theological with the historical order, but also from the inevitable human processes that keep divisions open once they have been made, and make them ever wider. Here, too, we must be aware of all the complexities. For example, almost all the divisions in the Church today have long enough histories to make them situations into which we have been born, not situations for which we are responsible. That does not make them any easier to end, but we shall make no progress if we treat them as wilful schisms in which one side is clearly in the right and the other has to yield to it.

But in that case, is the whole problem reduced to a question of expediency? Again, of course not. Now, as always, the nature of Christ's work shown forth by the Church demands *one* visible Church as its realization and its response to him; and one visible Church, whatever the varieties within it, demands one ministry and one faith. And there are indeed norms to help us towards realizing this unity as far as is possible in the historical order. I have dwelt several times on their complexity, for the chief danger seems to me to come from those who would over-simplify them, but they are there, and it is not beyond the wit of man, if he has the will, to use them in working forward to more visible unity.

All this has to be said in a Christian context, to Christians. But if a single point had to be put over in a secular context, it would be a simple one, namely, that it is impossible to talk about the Church without taking into account its constant recognition that it is not only an empirical reality but something more, which it is compelled to describe in theological terms. The Church therefore cannot and does not and will not try to justify its existence and its work in purely this-worldly terms. It questions the adequacy of these terms by its very existence and experience. And, conversely, if it should try to justify its existence only in this-worldly terms, it will abandon all reasons for existing in anything like its present form. There is a position from which the Christian cannot afford to retreat.

Now anyone who is ready to persevere this far through a series of 'Difficulties for Christian Belief' is obviously open enough to consider ways in which these difficulties might be alleviated. But to come this far is to have come a long way. Most of our contemporaries shy off the moment the word 'Church' is mentioned. They suppose that they know what it means and they do not like it. It has associations that so deter them that they are unwilling to open a conversation on the question, except to air their stereotype criticisms, let alone to sustain it. They are not prepared to wait patiently for alternative explanations because they feel that nothing can explain away what they think they see. There is an 'image' of the Church that gets in the way.

The material for this image is largely supplied by the Church of England, and as I am an Anglican, it is the Church of England I shall particularly have in mind in the rest of what I have to say. But it may also apply to other traditions, at least in part.

The Church is thought of, dismissed, criticized, resented, above all as an institution. Its apparent privilege, authority, formalism, its embodiment and perpetuation of the social conditions of a different age, all stand in the way of a serious consideration of the real issues, And the Church does little to dispel this misconception. Time and again, reading what tends to be printed in the Church newspapers and said in Church assemblies and conferences of one sort or another, one has the impression that having

jettisoned what put it in orbit in the first place, the
Church is above all concerned to stay still, or whirl round,
just as it is. It has resigned itself to being an organization,
and its interests and its business are primarily, to all
appearances, those of an organization: financial, adminis-
trative, social. It is bad form to snipe at the organization
by criticizing it from within; that is disloyalty to the
company. And, still in the terms of the business world,
the remedy being canvassed for present trouble is that
of providing a new 'image' for the Church. In the spring
of 1965, *The Times* carried a series of articles on new
trends in marketing groceries, one of which dealt with
the problems of a dated institution with a number of
rebellious, stubbornly independent, and unco-ordinated
sub-branches, and described attempts made to give the
concern a face-lift. Only with difficulty could one forget
that one was not reading just one more article about the
Church; it was, in fact, about the Co-op.

But the solution is not as easy as that. The signs of the
refusal of our contemporaries to identify themselves with
the organized life of the Church have been mounting so
rapidly in recent years that they cannot be ignored. The
number of infant baptisms has fallen sharply, the number
of those who go to church continues to decline. And above
all, there has been a catastrophic drop in the number of
candidates offering themselves for ordination, and an
increasing number are leaving the parish ministry after
ordination, through sheer dissatisfaction, frustration, and

a feeling that their work under the conditions imposed upon them is quite irrelevant.

Consequently, at the other extreme, there have been suggestions that have closely followed Dietrich Bonhoeffer's vision of the Church of the future, which ends his 'Outline for a Book' in *Letters and Papers from Prison*. The Church should sever its connections with the State, give away its endowments, scrap the parish system, and start a new life in the form of a servant.

The difficulty with such radical suggestions, even if they were altogether desirable, which is doubtful, is the virtual impossibility of putting them into practice. Whatever else the Church is, it is people, and changes that involve people cannot possibly be made to order, at the stroke of a pen. Moreover, no one who has ever worked within the framework of the Church in its present form will sneer at it, whatever its faults. For within that framework, at the parish level, even in the most unprepossessing parish, there are always countless unpublicized, almost unknown ways in which the Church really is being the body of Christ, composed of people as they are, helping people in the name of Christ as they are, doing the most difficult of all Christian work in the most difficult conditions. There is much that the parish ministry, within the parish framework, can still do. But it must realize that these potentialities are, and where the limitations lie.

Within the parish church it is, infuriatingly, possible to feel that there is a solidity about the external form of the life of the community, determined by its immediate history and the preferences of its members, which cannot and will not change, whatever may happen in the world outside. Church buildings, the liturgy, the organizations of the Church, all contribute to the feeling that the present life of the Church is its own justification, that there is all the time in the world, and that all the Church needs to do is to hold fast. But this really is an illusion; solidity of this sort is not the basis of the Church as the body of Christ—it is to rely on a security that is less than the ultimate security, and it distracts attention from the urgent task of reflection that is needed. The parish church and the parish system will not remain the same for ever. The writing is on the wall. The life of the parish church cannot be taken as self-justifying; all its features need to be questioned and challenged one by one, not accepted unthinkingly.

Here is the fatal weakness of the modern Church. Almost from top to bottom a real, urgent, constant concern for reflection upon its own nature, and that means theology, is lacking. The leading teachers and doctors of the Church are no longer to be found as they used to be in its bishops and priests. Theology is now being taught and written predominantly in the open settings of schools and universities. This in itself is a good, sound, healthy position; it is right that in a society like ours theology should hold a place where it can be in dialogue with other disciplines. But where the theologians have led, the Church has been reluctant to follow. The attempts of theology over the last one hundred and fifty years to come to grips with the problems raised by the discoveries achieved by the scientific method and the revolution in knowledge have inevitably taken it along unfamiliar paths, and instead of showing sympathy, the Church as an institution has all too often disowned and neglected theology, or even actively opposed it. Having sowed the wind, the Church is now beginning to reap the whirlwind, as the new generation of qualified graduates coming from universities and training colleges turn their back on an organized body that is so oblivious of the difficulties that its thought, attitude, and language presents to them.

The Church *must* take its theology seriously. We have seen that it is a society that cannot come to grips with the world around it, cannot justify itself to that world in purely this-worldly terms. It points to something more. But what that something more is is no longer obvious. It has to be explained. In this most difficult of periods the Church has to learn to be articulate about its *raison d'être*. All the problems that were so clearly stated in the first lecture are still real problems by the last. The generation's work has still to be done, and to be done by the Church. And one vital element in it will be the Church's reflection on what it means to be the Church, to

have had the history and the communal experience that
the Church has had.

If this reflection will lead to new expressions of
theology, it will also lead to new forms of Church life.
Church order and institutionalism are two very different
things, and the former can be developed to fulfil the
Church's needs without falling into the latter. What we
must look for and expect, as a consequence of thought
about the doctrine of the Church, is a development of
all sorts of new forms of Church life alongside the old
pattern, and the old pattern and its concern for self-
preservation must not be allowed to obscure the new.
There are books enough on how this development might
take shape; they simply need to be thought about, and
put into practice. The essentials of the question are clear
from two recent books, which have important insights to
offer, even if their findings cannot be transferred whole-
sale to the situation in this country. Writing in a preface
to Horst Symanowski's *The Christian Witness in an
Industrial Society*, Robert Starbuck says:

It is necessary to supplement the parish structures
with other structures more closely related to the complex, diffused patterns of a pluralist society . . . and to
supplement the parish ministry with other forms of the
ministry more closely related to the various callings of
man in the contemporary world.

And in the same vein, Harvey Cox argues:

The difficulty is that we are not moving from one stage of society in which a particular form of church life, the residential parish, was the characteristic form into a stage in which some other form of church life will replace it. The situation is far more complex. The key word to describe what is happening in our society is *differentiation*. We are moving into a stage in which we will need a widely differentiated range of different types of church organization to engage a society which is becoming differentiated at an accelerated rate.[1]

And he goes on to describe how in different parts of the country, in different levels of society, flexible, transitory forms of the Church will be needed to serve the needs of a flexible, mobile population, to develop alongside the old.

These are the central questions with which we are faced in a society without roots. What should be the form of the Church in the school, technical college, university, hospital, factory? How is the Church in these contexts to maintain a common focal point of worship and society among its members and yet be an outward-looking Church? One of the most popular clichés is that 'the Church is a servant'. But if that is so, what are its qualifications in a complicated, technological world, which is interested above all in skilled men and not in the well-meaning, unskilled amateur? Can the Church offer a coherent account of its status? Can its place be anywhere

[1] *The Secular City*, p. 157.

else than on the periphery, and if so, how? These questions call upon all the resources of the Christian community, from its theology to the particular knowledge and experience of its members in the spheres in which they live and work. And above all, they call for Christian unity.

The problem of the form of the Church in the modern world is not a specialist concern for those who have it as their own particular hobby-horse. It is everyone's concern, because if anything should have stood out from this whole discussion it is that all Christians, whether ordained or not, are equally the Church, and responsibility cannot be delegated to someone else, somewhere else.

He would be a hopeful man indeed who did not see continuing difficulties ahead. The problems of unity will long be with us, not so much perhaps in the old forms, for co-operation and understanding between the different traditions is developing at some levels at a rate unhoped-for twenty years ago. The real crisis is more likely to be in the tension between traditional attitudes to the Church and to Church life and more open ones, ready for exploration and experimentation, between the old and the new, between very different expressions of faith within the same tradition. And here the horizon is not perhaps so clear.

But in all the discussions, one thing must never be forgotten. It may well be that in some places, including our own country, the external fortunes of the Church will continue to decline, and force it to lose many of the characteristics by which we know it today. But this is of secondary importance, provided that the Church's future hopes centre on attempts to express its nature in a modest form, appropriate to the reality to which it bears witness and the society in which it lives. If it is faithful to the God who called it into being and to the witness that it is its mission to bear, it has nothing to fear.[1]

---

[1] I have been helped by the books, prefixed by an asterisk, listed in the Reading List, p. 150.

Reading List

Karl Barth (trans. E. C. Hoskyns), *The Epistle to the Romans*. O.U.P., 1933.

Saul Bellow, *Henderson the Rain King*. Weidenfeld & Nicolson, 1959.

Dietrich Bonhoeffer (trans. R. H. Fuller), *Letters and Papers from Prison*, rev. edn., S.C.M. Press, 1956; Fontana Books, 1959.

John Braine, *Room at the Top*. Eyre & Spottiswoode, 1957.

Albert Camus (trans. J. O'Brien), *The Fall*. Hamish Hamilton, 1957.

Harvey Cox, *The Secular City*, S.C.M. Press, 1965.

Gregory Dix, *The Shape of the Liturgy*. Dacre Press, 1945.

Ernest Gellner, 'The Crisis in the Humanities and the Mainstream of Philosophy', in *Crisis in the Humanities*. Penguin Books, 1964.

William Golding, *Lord of the Flies*. Faber, 1954.

S. L. Greenslade, *Schism in the Early Church*. S.C.M. Press, 1964

A. T. Hanson, *Beyond Anglicanism*. Darton, Longman & Todd, 1965.

John Knox, *The Church and the Reality of Christ*. Collins, 1963.

Lesslie Newbigin, *The Household of God*, S.C.M. Press, 1964.

Rudolph Otto (trans. J. W. Harvey), *Das Heilige* (*The Idea of the Holy*), 2nd edn. O.U.P., 1950; Penguin, 1959.

Albert Schweitzer), *The Quest of the Historical Jesus*, 3rd edn. Black, 1954.

Horst Symanowski, *The Christian Witness in an Industrial Society*. Collins, 1966.

Alec R. Vidler, *Plain Man's Guide to Christianity*. Heinemann, 1936.

Helen Waddell, *Peter Abelard*. Constable, 1933; 4th impr. 1944.

Index

I. BIBLICAL REFERENCES

II. NAMES